VOX LIBRI

VOX LIBRI

CASS LAUER

NEW DEGREE PRESS

VOX LIBRI

ISBN   979-8-88504-543-8 *Paperback*
        979-8-88504-869-9 *Kindle Ebook*
        979-8-88504-659-6 *Ebook*

monachopsis (n)—the subtle but persistent feeling of being out of place, as maladapted to your surroundings as a seal on a beach, lumbering and clumsy, huddled in the company of other misfits, dreaming of life in your natural habitat, a place where you'd be fluidly, brilliantly, effortlessly at home.

fitzcarraldo (n)—a random image that becomes lodged deep in your brain—maybe washed there by a dream, or smuggled inside a book, or planted during a casual conversation—which then grows into a wild and impractical vision that keeps scrambling around in your head, itching for a chance to leap headlong into reality.

—*THE DICTIONARY OF OBSCURE SORROWS* BY JOHN KOENIG

To the girl in the attic—

You did what was necessary to get where you are. Don't forget to be proud.

CONTENTS

——

AUTHOR'S NOTE

———

"Hwæt. We Gardena in geardagum, þeodcyninga, þrym
gefrunon, hu ða æþelingas ellen fremedon…"

(BEOWULF, LINES 1-3).

Standing at the head of the class, neck stretched tall, and
arms behind his back, my professor punctuated the verse.
"þæt wæs god cyning" (*Beowulf,* line 11).

Not a single one of us understood the words pouring
from his mouth. But it was in fact English, he reassured us.
More accurately, it was an ancestor of the English language
we know and use today. Professor Boyd revealed the idea of
language families and defined that field of study as etymology. Whereas this was just another day in another lecture
for my peers, I'd discovered a whole new world to explore.

The lesson was illuminating; such as learning the life
story of your favorite person and how they got to be who
they are. You trace the path of their history to discover the
growth within that person, or in this case the language. And

in doing so, you appreciate them more deeply than you ever had before.

However, when thinking of my own history, there were gaps. Reflecting back, this makes total sense as mental health disorders—in my case, anxiety and depression—have a large effect on memory (Schweizer, 2018). But even through the blur, I do remember this deep-rooted desire to be understood. The clearest way to communicate—words.

Words have always been important to me, and I always paid attention to word choice. The best-used word could clear up any misunderstanding or create the strongest connection. So when it came time to go to college, I knew I wanted to study words. But even with this newfound admiration of etymology, I couldn't help but notice even more gaps. Holes. Feelings ineffectually being explained by words that didn't quite fit. Spaces longing to be filled where the English language—both past and present—fell short.

Not long after, while attending a summer writing conference at UMASS Amherst, I stumbled on a blog called *The Dictionary of Obscure Sorrows* (Koenig, 2009). In it was a series of completely made-up words by John Koenig piecing together existing prefixes, suffixes, and roots to give name to unique yet often universal feelings and phenomena: the sudden awareness that you will die; a hypothetical conversation you have in your head; the desire to care less about things; and my all-time favorite, the disappointment of being unable to fly.

Here, laid out in front of me, were the missing pieces! And for the rest of the week, I continued using Koenig's words as prompts.

Returning home for my final year of college, *The Dictionary of Obscure Sorrows* stuck in my head like a song on repeat, and I needed a story for my senior writing project. But when you're a storyteller who can't remember their own stories to share, creating something out of nothing is a woeful experience. So, painfully, I created characters, picked a setting, and tried wedging someone else's etymology into my own. But I quickly grew uninspired and the project fell to the wayside. And because mental illness prevented me from finishing school, I never had to turn it in.

Years passed and it remained unfinished. My firecracker-loud anxiety disorder created a comfortable home for itself and I grew complacent in a job I liked enough that allowed me to make noise louder than those in my head. I'd roll out of bed around 2 p.m., walk a few dogs, work from 3:30-9:30 p.m., grab dinner from wherever—usually McDonald's—and then binge comfort shows to drown out my brain. My days passed as if I'd never spent years studying creative writing and the English language. However, I'd sometimes find myself in my dark bedroom, the glow from my computer like a spotlight as I'd scroll through my old writing.

The occasional revisiting of my senior writing project acted as a reminder that at some point, I wanted to be an author. At some point, that was an active personal truth. Otherwise, why would I have taken on a debt so colossal it demanded monthly offerings like a Greek deity? But whenever I tried thinking back, there was nothing but TV static. The connection was tenuous at best.

While the last decade has seen significantly more conversation surrounding mental wellness, this deep-rooted—characteristically American—bootstrapping ideal remains. Specifically, along the lines of this lone-wolf mentality; that no one can help "fix you" or change your circumstances, and you need to figure everything out on your own. And while it is the individual's responsibility to take initiative, for some—especially those living with mental illness—it's not feasible to make progress without assistance.

The difficulty one faces when trying to assemble a life is seldom expressed when living with an infrequently treated mental illness. Without the ability to reflect on one's past, to be able to see where you started, it's near impossible to build anything without a clearly established foundation. This becomes even more aggravating when the individual watches those around them succeeding at creating a sustainable life but not being able to break down the basic step-by-step of how they did so—as I experienced.

On top of my inability to process as my peers did due to the ever-clanging pots and pans in my ears, even my complacency was becoming unsustainable. I was experiencing both severe burnout and physical pain from work, resulting in my departure without any established direction or prospects.

But once I had a moment to rest, I allowed myself the opportunity to slow down and catch my breath. And as the anxiety fell to that of a low hum—still audible, but easy enough to regularly ignore—I again stumbled upon *The Dictionary of Obscure Sorrows*. I was again reminded of who I wanted to be.

During this time, a friend's mother—who I'd come to see as both a friend and a mentor figure—reached out. She explained she was participating in a life coach certification program and needed to put in a certain number of training hours to complete the process. She then asked if I'd be her guinea pig. We met for a weekly hour across a few months, both in-person and over the phone, while she explained how to create a basic foundation to build a life upon. I can assuredly state, that had she not put these steps into words, I would still be lost.

Not long afterward, I dove head first into freelance literary editing. I joined the Book Creators team and worked alongside many first-time authors in the early stages of their book writing journey. For years, I've met people with diverse experiences who all joined the Book Creators program for one reason—to share a story. They all wanted to reach out to other people in hopes of forming a connection—whether through education, commiseration, or simply entertainment—all through my most-loved vehicle. Words.

Oftentimes, it takes seeing other people express their stories to understand how we can discover a direction for ourselves. Putting words to our experiences also gives us the opportunity to make sense of our past and find a better way forward. Without language—Sign Language and nonverbal communication included—humankind is doomed to drift around listlessly. It allows us to cross chasms of loneliness to find comfort in others and gives us the opportunity to recognize a universal Human Experience. After all, we're all born babbling.

These pages tell the tale of Etta, a lonely copywriter in search of assurance, companionship, and a life worthy of no distractions. But as she finds complacency in the routine of adulthood, she quickly loses herself in the pages of *Vox Libri*, a mystical book that causes its reader to have hallucinations. While unearthing her own voice, others are louder—including the book. Etta must resist passivity so as not to lose her humanness.

Vox Libri is my love letter to the English language itself and to those who are self-identified word nerds and book lovers. It is my effort to find the right words and share them with the public. But more specifically, this is for those of us who believed we didn't have a purpose, those who've fought

PROLOGUE

Before you is a path. It's wide and lined with trees. The sun breaks through the clearing and warms the earth. Next to you are your four friends. They joke, tell stories, and discuss all the adventures they want to have. Together, you hop, skip, run, and dance down the path. Everything is well. Everything is good.

As you go farther down, you and your friends discover a fork in the path. It is just as bright as the path you're already on with just as many trees. No sign explains where it leads, so you consult with your friends on what to do.

Four of the five, including you, agree your journey is perfect as is. And while your fifth friend agrees, curiosity gets the better of them. They decide to take the new path.

At the fork, the four of you hug your friend goodbye. You wish them luck and pray to see them again at the end of the road. They go their own way, and you continue along with the rest of your friends.

The journey continues. Now that there are only four of you, the path narrows slightly to just big enough to comfortably fit four. The trees grow taller and denser. There's more shade than there once was, but you all still joke. You still tell stories. You still discuss the adventures you want to have. And now, you wonder what your fifth friend is exploring.

Soon enough, you happen upon another fork. It's slightly more shaded than the last path with a few more trees but still no directional signs. You all discuss what to do.

Three of the five, including you, agree your journey is still going strong. Why mess with a good thing? And while your fourth friend agrees, excitement gets the better of them. They decide to take the new path.

So the three of you hug your friend goodbye. You wish them luck and pray to run into them again in the future. They go their own way, and the three of you continue along.

As the three of you follow your path, it shrinks again. So much so that if you were to run into your old friends, the five of you would no longer be able to walk side by side. The trees have also grown again. They are taller and thicker with less gaps for the sun to break through. It is a little cooler. But the three of you push on—telling jokes and stories while discussing your future adventures and wondering what your fourth and fifth friend are doing.

Eventually, you come upon another fork. It's slimmer than the other two forks. It's darker than the other two forks. And there still isn't a sign. The three of you argue over what to do.

"Why would we go down a new path?" you explain. "Why change course?"

"We don't know what's down that way," your one friend illustrates.

"What if it doesn't get better than this?" your other friend shouts, pointing to the new path. "What if it gets worse?"

"But what if it gets better?" you cry.

Two of you agree you are comfortable on the current path.

But your third friend lets restlessness get the better of them. They decide to take the new path.

Before they depart, the two of you hug them goodbye. You wish them luck and pray to see them again later.

You turn to your last remaining friend and ask, "Do you think we'll see them again?"

They look back at you and say, "We haven't seen the others yet."

As the two of you forge ahead, the path feels cramped. The trees stand closer together, one right after the other. They reach up toward the sky, taller than any building you've ever seen. The sun tries desperately to warm the earth, but the trees won't let it. Instead, you feel a soft, cool glow, the kind you can only find deep in the forest.

As it has before, the path comes to another fork. It's the tightest of them all but the darkest of them all. It's slightly overgrown and difficult to see. Worse yet, there's still no sign. You turn toward your only friend and consider what to do.

Your friend is nervous. They are afraid. They wonder how your other friends are faring. They wonder if this is the last fork in the road. Your friend lets anxiety get the better of them. They decide to take the new path.

You try to fight back, to get them to stay, but you're tired. You hug your friend goodbye. You wish them luck and pray to see them again someday.

After pushing for some time, your own path becomes overgrown. The trees are the thickest they've been. The sun can no longer shine through. It's getting harder to see the way, and it's getting colder. You're exhausted and alone. You're sad and mourning the loss of your friends. You miss their company. You let melancholy get the better of you. You stop where you are and sit. You make no plans to trek on.

CHAPTER 1

Etta walked hard to work. She'd only just passed the bluish Queen Anne with the wrap-around porch, two minutes behind schedule. The frigid wind broke through to her chest, even though she'd made a point to wear extra layers that day. Her heels dug into the pavement as she pressed onward, her clenched fist tightening around the strap of her backpack. Etta was too new to be a few minutes late again.

Burying her nose in her scarf, her mind cycled through the reasons why she wouldn't call Northampton a city. Long ago, someone defined it by the size of its population. And technically Northampton met those criteria. But Etta had been to New York, Chicago, and Boston many times, and she conclusively decided that Northampton, Massachusetts was not a city by any logical person's standards.

Nearing the stone building, Etta reached for the heavy door and its icy handle. Grateful for the gloves her mother knitted her for Christmas, she pulled the door open, ripped off her gloves, and then used one to wipe the fog off her glasses. Her steps echoed on the stairwell as she made a mental note to send a lovely text of gratitude to her mom during lunch.

She walked onto the second floor and passed both Parts-of-Speech Terach's and A-through-H Agnes's cubicles, politely returning their smiles before tossing her jacket and backpack on the extra chair in her cubicle corner. She plopped in front of her computer, and the chair swiveled as the computer fan whirred and the screen hummed to life. Etta blinked repeatedly, hoping to get her eyes to focus after rubbing them too hard. When her vision finally cleared, she pulled up her online Scrabble games and played "cappuccino" for seventeen points against Sentences-Phrases-and-Clauses Denise.

Settling deeper into her chair, Etta decided her cubicle could have been nicer if she put more effort into it. But as it stood, she was nonplussed by the drab gray, pushpin-cushioned wall. She considered hanging that picture of her mother from the family vacation before moving to Northampton and even her younger sister's ballet company photo as she chipped off bits of the peel-and-stick wood from the corner of her desk. Either tactic would be a vast improvement, and maybe it'd help her focus more on the work tasks delegated by Copy Chief Valeska.

On her typical Saturday trip to Amherst, Etta decided Valeska was very pleasant, both as a boss and as a human being. While standing in line at her regular coffee shop, Etta reflected back to the previous afternoon. Valeska bopped between cubicles, offering up a quick reminder that they had only two hours left until the weekend. Enthusiastic, seemingly by nature, she even made a point to stop for longer at Etta's and ask about her weekend plans. She didn't have much to share, but it solidified the idea Valeska was just plain pleasant.

Etta opened an email from said Copy Chief. The copywriter meeting was scheduled for tomorrow at two. Everyone would crowd around the conference table to discuss the progress on the latest flashcard projects and essentially indulge in their work egos. Denise and Terach would brag about how quickly they were working through their flashcards while Agnes would try redirecting the conversation to her family. Meanwhile, Valeska would thoughtfully serve coffee from The Roasted Bean—or The Burnt Bean, as Etta pseudo-affectionately named it. But Etta admitted the only thing that came from these meetings was an opportunity to stare down her online Scrabble enemies.

The day continued and Etta kept catching herself Scrabbling instead of working. She beat Denise after editing *luxation*—the dislocation of an anatomical part—and started a new game with a random player instead of moving on to her next word. Her opponent played *coffee* for fourteen points. She cursed the stranger for having a strong start, and the word played on a repetitive loop in her head. It was warm and smooth and flooded her thoughts. But the word also had teeth; dull ones that were mostly harmless but still a bit like a teething toddler. Before the word faded away, she pulled out the overly scratched notebook with its overly bent cover from her backpack, wrote it down, and then opened up *Oxford English Dictionary*'s online database to figure out its etymology.

Etta loved getting lost in the origins of words and language. The history of a word and its evolution through time made the past and its people seem not as distant from the present. She peeked out of her cubicle, scanning the office for Valeska, and then wheeled back to her computer. The homepage to the *OED* reflected off her glasses as she typed the six letters into the search bar. She clicked her pen as well as the first link and then began scratching words and timelines into her notebook:

221. Coffee—a drink made by infusion or decoction from the seeds of a shrub, roasted and ground; extensively used as a beverage and acting as a moderate stimulant—from the Italian word caffe stemming from the Turkish word kahveh deriving from the Arabic word qahwah, which originally meant "wine" but the coffee plant was originally grown in the Kaffa region of Ethiopia, which exported the beans to Arabia, which brought the beans to Europe sometime in the 1500s.

Sitting back in her chair, Etta's eyes lingered on the newest entry, watching history retroactively unfold as great civilizations met and traded with one another. But her job wasn't to understand the significance of the words she edited. It didn't matter to Brain Train whether she knew *kindergarten* came from the translated German phrase "children's garden" coined by the educationalist Friedrich Fröbel in 1840; and that because of his work and research with preschool-aged children, singing, dancing, and play—even gardening—were finally understood to be crucial educational tools due to the developmental effects they had on young children. Thus permeating popular culture enough for Etta to have the opportunity to go to kindergarten nearly 150 years later. And how kismet was that?

But overromanticizing a piece of the past was not her assigned task. All Brain Train copywriters had to create English grammar and vocab flashcards with the clearest, most concise definitions possible—Etta handled I through Q.

And so, Brain Train's *coffee* was plainly "a dark brown drink made from ground coffee beans and boiled water." Their readers didn't want a distraction. They didn't need to fill up an overabundance of time. They needed the definition so they could flip the flashcard over and then move on to the next one.

"Don't let Valeska see you were late," Etta heard Parts-of-Speech's pseudo-whisper.

"Snitches get stitches, Ter," a second voice joked before passing the entrance of Etta's cubicle. R-through-Z Cane flashed a friendly smile at her with a quick, "Morning," before disappearing into their own.

Officially reaching her morning distraction limit, Etta let in a big breath of air, held it for a moment, and then released it as slowly as she could manage. With as much intent as she could muster, she exited out of both the *OED* website and her Scrabble games. *Lyre*—"a musical instrument with strings used especially in Ancient Greece"—laid starkly against her screen.

Lyric. Lyrical, she thought, as she scribbled 222. *Lyre* into her notebook before putting it back in her backpack. She typed out "a stringed instrument used especially in Ancient Greece" and tried moving on to the next word.

"Hey!" Valeska interrupted, knocking on the wall of Etta's cubicle. "I'm heading over to Olympic Deli for lunch. Want to come?"

Etta politely returned her boss's smile, eager to find any other excuse not to do work. "Yeah, okay."

"Great! Agnes is driving. She said she'd meet us out front."

Etta nodded through a tight-lipped smile failing to ignore the swift, invisible fist jabbing her square in the stomach.

Etta stared out the backseat window at the brick buildings of not-city Northampton as Agnes flew over every pothole. She was a plump, older woman with a faded German accent who constantly found a way to bring up her personal history in almost every conversation—moving from West Germany in the late sixties, going to night school for English while working day shifts at a diner, anything and everything about her grandchildren. Valeska smiled and laughed along to all of Agnes's stories while Etta mostly stayed quiet in fear of misunderstanding her.

Etta pulled off her gloves and felt the crisp air stinging her fingers. Agnes's heater wasn't what it used to be, but how could she get rid of the station wagon that carted all of her *jungen* to school and soccer practice?

It wasn't that Etta necessarily disliked children. Nor did she hold it against Agnes for adoring her grandchild or judge Valeska for being excited over her wife's pregnancy. Young children just weren't her favorite kind of people. It was as if Etta didn't have the gene that taught someone how to engage with anyone under the age of thirteen. Etta tuned out the conversation from the front seat and quickly sent the text to her mother.

"What about you, Odette?" Agnes pried—her Ws sounding more like Vs—as she pulled the car into a parking space. "Do you have any great *kinder* stories?"

Her only sister was freshly nineteen and trying to break out as a professional ballerina in Chicago; her oldest cousin was preoccupied with "living life to the fullest" ever since he caught his girlfriend cheating on him; and her youngest cousin was now fifteen. *Kinder* interactions were recently few and far between.

"Well," Etta began, putting her gloves back on. "When my youngest cousin was ten, he called me out for patronizing him at a family party. And actually used the word patronizing."

The car grew quiet. She couldn't see their reactions, but Etta could feel the strained amusement settle on their faces.

Luckily, Agnes clunked the car against the curb and into a spot on the street.

Stepping out of the car, the group made their way toward the front door of the Olympic Deli. The smell of Lysol and mayo greeted the women along with an older man with a graying beard behind the counter. He took their orders and told them to pick a table. He'd bring their sandwiches out in a moment.

Valeska led the group to a window table that wobbled if Agnes put too much weight on her side. Etta again stared through the window, past the yellowing vinyl blinds, and watched as the cars drove under the bridge as Agnes began asking one too many questions about Valeska's home situation. Etta didn't feel comfortable enough or close enough to her boss to ask if Agnes was being too intrusive and too insensitive. Nor could she think of anything to contribute to the conversation in hopes of redirecting focus.

Nothing much was going on in her personal life to speak about. Etta regularly woke up, walked to work, pretended to work, walked back to her apartment, and then waited for her roommate to come home and tease her about being a couch potato and needing to get out more. But she did get out. Every weekend. To Amherst, specifically. Etta would pack her bag, hop on the bus, and then sit at an indie bookstore for hours. That may not have been exactly what her roommate had meant by "getting out," but in Etta's mind, it still counted.

"Thank you!" Copy Chief chirped to the deli man placing the sandwiches on the table. "Agnes, could you pass us some napkins?"

Agnes pulled a stack out of the holder and separated it into three smaller piles, placing each one next to everyone's food. Etta smiled out of politeness and proceeded to pick at the edges of the bread.

"So, Odette," Agnes began, putting on the embarrassing and intrusive smile an older aunt gives right before she asks something too personal. "Is there a special man in your life?" Etta snorted, shaking her head faster than was absolutely necessary. "Not unless you count my roommate and his cat." She laughed, thinking about her roommate sitting on the couch marathoning Monty Python all day.

"Oh!" Agnes replied, clapping her hands together. "You're living with someone! Valeska, isn't that nice? It's serious?"

Etta looked to Valeska for help, but she only offered a side-eye and tight-lipped smile. It wasn't much, but it comforted Etta knowing her boss understood without needing an explanation. She looked down at her sandwich as she answered.

"Well, Cleese gets a little frisky and will rub up against me while Sam sits and watches *Holy Grail*."

Agnes's face sank, and Valeska awkwardly laughed at Etta's failed attempt at wit. The entire deli quieted down as the embarrassment filled whatever space was left in Etta's stomach that her sandwich hadn't occupied.

"Cleese is the... He's the cat," Etta explained. "And nothing is going on between Sam and me. He actually has a date tonight with a guy outside of the entire Monty Python cast."

Agnes laughed a little, reaching across the table to playfully push Etta's shoulder. "Oh, you kidder, you!"

CHAPTER 2

———

Seated in her swivel chair, Etta clamped down on her bottom lip, impatiently tapping her foot. Locked in a staring contest with her jacket as if challenging it to a duel, Etta glared intensely. The grounds: the frozen landscape of Northampton, Massachusetts. The distance: the twenty-minute walk from Brain Train to her apartment.

She never really despised her walk home. For the most part, the time spent alone was enjoyable. It was nice to walk through the residential area and gaze at the series of houses so characteristically Olde Massachusetts. Each one stood two to three stories tall, some with peaks or towers and some with beautiful wrap-around porches. Her favorite homes were the more ornate Queen Annes of multiple colors. Her favorite had a sharp tower with a third-story porch and was only a block off her path. In the warmer weather, Etta often found herself wandering the neighborhood to kill time.

However, these winter months contributed to Etta's severe frigidity—both in temperature and demeanor. Winter always had this effect but never this starkly before. They could get bleak back in New Jersey but never chill-you-straight-to-the-bone-while-four-feet-of-snow-blocked-your-front-door bleak.

But while waiting for her jacket to either apologize or catch fire, she quickly realized the true offender. No number of layers would ever stand a chance against a bleak New England winter.

"Psst!"

Etta spotted Valeska reenacting the promo picture of *Mrs. Doubtfire* at the entrance of her cubicle, smiling back at her. Her height never failed to take Etta by surprise, and she half-expected her boss to be standing on a stool until she stepped forward and sat at the edge of the desk. Valeska looked so warm wrapped up in her fluffy red scarf, matching earmuffs, and floor-length khaki overcoat.

"Is something incredibly interesting about your jacket? Will it start to sing and dance?" Her laughter warmed the small enclosure. The ability to make anyone feel comfortable at any time appeared to come so naturally to her boss. Etta assumed it came with practice.

"I'm trying to put off being cold," she lamented, dreading the inevitable outdoor exposure.

"I think it'd work a little better if you actually put the coat on."

"Yeah. That's very accurate." Etta chuckled, feeling the tension in her body give way. Again, she felt more settled than just moments before. "But once I get outside and start walking, it's not really going to matter anyway."

Valeska flipped her keys into her hands and then twirled them around her finger. She appeared so effortlessly cool. In the few months Etta had worked at Brain Train, she couldn't recall a single moment of Valeska boiling over with any ounce of discontent. As she wondered how her boss remained constantly collected, Valeska offered her a ride home.

"Are you sure?" Etta hesitated, almost waiting for Valeska to revoke the invitation. She didn't want to impose, especially on her boss who'd already spent an entire lunch break with her.

"Completely positive!" Valeska's voice jumped up several octaves, more enthusiastic than usual. "I promise. It is no problem at all."

Etta quickly gathered her things, nearly jumping into the jacket she'd spent so long staring at. Valeska led the way down the stairs to her four-door, and they set off for home.

Hanging from the rearview mirror, an unpolished crystal swung back and forth. Etta watched it sway before stopping it with her hand to get a better look when the car stopped under a streetlight.

"Jenny's kind of into the whole New Age thing," Valeska explained. Etta had only met Valeska's wife once before, but she understood this almost instantly from the many rings on her fingers and crystals and charms around her neck. "She's all about feng shui and burning incense to boost our positive energy before the baby gets here. She smudged the nursery last week, and it still smells like sage no matter what we do. Thankfully our neighbors are cool with it."

"That's nice." Letting go of the crystal, Etta settled back in her seat. She appreciated Valeska's openness, particularly about this spiritual stuff. Back home, she was side-eyed anytime she walked in or out of the New Age store.

"Sam hung up a mirror by our front door and plugs in one of those desk fountains every now and then," Etta continued. "That's about the extent of our feng shui-y-ness. But I used to mess around with a tarot deck when I was younger.

I probably still have it somewhere. Probably at the bottom of one of the boxes I never unpacked after moving in."

"Hasn't it been like eight months?"

"Ten." Etta sighed. She paused, taking a cautious moment to decide whether to share the next bit. But at this point, she felt so at ease that she internally shrugged. "I remember you mentioning something about meeting up with your... um... donor sometime around my fifth week."

Valeska chuckled as she pulled up to Etta's apartment. "Jenny refuses to have a tarot deck anywhere near the apartment anymore. She had this phase in her life where she kept pulling The Tower and Nine of Swords. Destruction and despair became somewhat of a running joke after a while."

Etta nodded along completely understanding Jenny's qualms. It wasn't for superstitious reasons. Tarot cards weren't oujia boards. They couldn't act as a swinging door for evil spirits. From Etta's own experiences, she simply noticed the cards would tell her the same thing after a while. And what's the point of asking the deck where you're going to be if it's always in the same place?

Etta reached for her backpack from the floor of the car. "I always got The Hermit, Three of Swords, and..." She stopped to consider. "Four of Pentacles reversed."

"I'm not as well-versed as my wife. What's that mean again?"

"Being stuck, I guess." With a tight-lipped smile and a low hum in her ear, Etta opened the car door. "So now I'm in Northampton." She climbed out of the car, turning toward her boss one last time. "Thanks again for the ride. I really appreciate it."

Valeska threw up a wave before pulling away. Because one goodbye couldn't be enough, Etta returned the gesture as she made her way toward the house. The water-stained siding left by the recently chopped-down pine that blocked Etta's bedroom window was barely noticeable in the moonlight. In its place sat an empty planter on a stump surrounded by frozen mulch.

Etta was grateful she lived on the second floor of a two-family home versus that four-floor brownstone she originally looked at. She was most grateful for the comparably limited number of steps leading to her apartment door. Between her walk to work and the two staircases she needed to climb before reaching her stodgy, unkempt cubicle, she always found herself out of breath and questioning why her many years of living in hilly neighborhoods hadn't prepared her for a twenty-minute walk and two flights of stairs. Thinking it over, Etta admitted her cubicle wasn't actually that disheveled. She did keep it rather orderly considering her flighty headspace. Realistically, her brain was only a tad erratic, and her cubicle was only a little shabby. But not too shabby. Just a little.

Her apartment, on the other hand, was quite airy and contemporary, considering it was housed in a not-impeccably-kept-up home. But it only felt that way because of the framed photographs or the Modernists prints orderly hung on every wall hiding the stark white paint. Or maybe it was the oversized red leather couch, which Sam bought off of his college roommate, sitting next to the sliding glass door. But it was most likely the plug-in desk fountain sitting on an end table under the mirror hanging as soon as you walked through the door.

No matter which way she looked at it, her apartment was comfy. And currently empty. And nearly silent. Besides the plane flying overhead and the tea kettle of her landlord in the downstairs apartment, the room was still. Tossing her keys next to the unflowing desk fountain, her body hiccupped as something swatted at her ankle. Snapping her head to the floor, she spotted the gray-striped culprit walking away from the entryway.

Cleese wasn't an unpleasant housecat, but he wasn't trustworthy. Especially after having chewed through and emptied an entire box of her favorite crackers. Granted, Sam cleaned up the mess and bought her another box, but Etta's and Cleese's relationship became strained and continued to strain considering how often he liked to sadistically sneak up on her when she wasn't expecting it.

Etta ignored Cleese as he smugly slunk away. She walked into the kitchenette and swung open the refrigerator door. The cool air stung her cheeks but wasn't strong enough to penetrate the layers she had yet to take off. If it wasn't so suspicious looking, she would consider buying a ski mask. But she'd never gone skiing before and didn't plan on doing so in the near future. For the moment, she was too concerned with her empty stomach and wished to remedy that first.

Luckily, they had leftover pizza. And not only did heating it up in the oven mean no uneven microwave cooking, but extra warmth while waiting for the old radiators Sam turned off to kick in.

After fifteen fast minutes, Etta plopped on the couch with her pizza. Cleese jumped off as soon as she sat and then pussyfooted toward Sam's room in contempt. Etta mockingly wiggled her head, pleased by Cleese's absence.

But with the room empty, Etta grew uncomfortable. The near-silence became increasingly louder by the moment. The second hands of both clocks—one in the living room and the other in the kitchen—were unsynchronized and off-beat. Which made sense. She never thought too deeply about it before, but the kitchen clock was always a few minutes faster, so of course, they wouldn't be in or on time.

However, as the seconds ticked by, the clocks became louder and more disquieting. The dead air filled her ears like a balloon about to burst or a bellow shoved into her ear canal, pumped until the pressure was too much. A chill ran through Etta's body before she snatched the remote and turned on the television. With a steadying breath, she picked up from where she left off marathoning *Buffy the Vampire Slayer* reruns and managed to relax. Several hours and a short nap later, Sam walked into the apartment.

"Fun night?" He almost laughed.

"The best." Etta stretched out, her arms and head hanging over the edge of the couch now viewing Sam upside down. "And you?"

"It was pleasant," Sam replied with a giddy smile on his face as he put his keys next to Etta's and then unzipped his jacket. Etta watched as he nearly danced through the living room toward his bedroom. Pausing at the door, he turned toward her and pursed his lips. His eyes shifted from side to side as the corners of his mouth pulled into a tight smile, clearly toying with the idea of sharing the events of his night. But Sam's face then collapsed in on itself and his head shuddered, deciding otherwise.

"Okay, well, I'm gonna go to bed," he teased. "Goodnight, Miss Odette!"

"You're giving me details tomorrow!" Etta called after him. Sitting up, she adjusted her glasses before making her way to the trashcan.

CHAPTER 3

———

At the top of the legal pad were the letters S, W, I, J, K, H, and M. Down the side, Etta scribbled the letters F, E, A, and C, followed by a list of possible words she could play in her Scrabble game after the meeting. Valeska and Agnes stood toward the head of the table exchanging baby stories as Denise and Terach found their seats.

"Terry! That's so bad!" Denise boomed, pulling her cardigan tighter around her rounded body. The two laughed as Terach shrugged his shoulders.

"Don't blame me," he began, pulling his wheely chair in closer. "I heard that one on Fallon last night. Plus, that's what you get for taking forever to make a Scrabble move."

"I'm working on it. You're gonna be blown away by the word I have in store for you!" Denise laughed. "Speaking of blown away, Odette got me real good the other day."

He nodded his head approvingly while softly golf clapping in Etta's direction. She smiled politely in return, not knowing exactly how to respond.

"Okay, guys!" Valeska began, still gleaming from whatever story Agnes told and raising her voice to catch the room's attention. R-through-Z Cane nudged through the closing door, flashing Valeska an apologetic smile before flinging their leather aviator jacket on the back of the empty seat next to Etta. Valeska sat at the end of the large, round table, leaving Cane and their jacket in Etta's direct line of vision. She knew people loved *Top Gun*, but she never realized people would love it enough to own and wear merch for it.

"We're gonna start in a few seconds, so get comfortable!"

Valeska drew in everyone's attention by beginning the meeting with praise. For the first time in her eight years as Copy Chief, the team was producing definitions ahead of schedule, meaning the copywriters could move on to the next flashcard topic—verbal analogies. She smiled even wider than usual and danced in her seat while sharing something about extra review time for any necessary changes. A quiet rumble of laughter spread throughout the table from the other copy editors feeding off of Valeska's energy. Laughing to herself, Etta jotted out possible Scrabble plays in the margin of her notes.

She looked up from her pad as Cane peered over at her writing through the corner of their eye. Leaning back in her chair, Etta crossed her arms. Irritated they were invading her personal space, Etta waited for Cane to catch her glaring. But Etta concluded Cane wasn't skilled at gaze detection after they turned their head back to Valeska.

Etta looked Cane up and down. At least what she could see of them. Even never having stood next to them, Etta could still determine Cane was tall, solely by their erect posture and the length of their arms. Their boss's voice fell to a steady hum and Etta watched as Cane cracked their fingers, pressing their knuckles down with only their thumb. With each snap, Etta's focus grew more intent and her eyes more strained. Cane rolled their shoulders and gently stretched their arms in front of themself, the cuffs of their button-down passing their elbows. Their short, dark hair touched the top of their back as they let their head fall back.

"And with that," Valeska said, interrupting Etta's engrossing distraction. She looked across the table, spotting Agnes shooting her a knowing glance. "You should all receive a personal memo from me within the week, and the staff dinner will be on the twenty-seventh—giving us a nice break halfway through the rest of our work!"

The copy editors clapped for Valeska—which seemed odd to Etta—and capped their pens before heading out of the conference room. Moving more slowly than usual, Agnes caught Etta's eye again, flashing the same embarrassing smile from the deli before taking her exit.

"Any particular reason why *kashmir* was written down on the corner of your notebook?" Cane asked, sitting deeper in their chair and turning to face Etta. She paused, startled by the interaction. Acutely aware of how many seconds had passed, Etta blinked out a reply.

"I'm going to play it in an online Scrabble game and then look up the definition online," she reluctantly admitted, thinking of a snarky comment two seconds too late.

Cane pursed their lips while nodding in what seemed like feigned interest. Etta pushed her seat back and made to leave.

"You can't play it."

"What? Why?" Her eyes snapped back to the top of the page. They were all there—the K, the S, the M, H, I—and she knew the rest were on the board thinking back to Denise's earlier *clear* and her own *suburb*. How would Cane know?

"It's a proper noun," they plainly replied.

"But it's a kind of scarf," Etta defended. Throwing her notepad down and pulling her seat back toward the table,

Etta had her pen ready. Cane shook their head and smiled, pulling themself in as well.

"Well, yeah, but then you're spelling it wrong." Gesturing to Etta's pen, Cane slipped it from Etta's fingers when she took too long. They scratched out some letters underneath her note. "Cashmere is made from the wool of some long-haired goats that live in the Himalayas. The area is called Kashmir. Spelled like the Led Zeppelin song. Like how you spelled it."

"Huh," Etta mulled, leaning back in her chair as Cane stood up. Her face grew tighter with perplexity by the second.

"Is that what the song's about?" Etta asked, her voice lilting higher, as Cane reached the door. "As in the location, not the scarf..."

Cane slowly turned back toward Etta, their hand gripping the open doorway, and grinned. "Yeah, I'm pretty sure it's about the Buddhist monks in the area. Not the scarf."

"Huh." Etta stood up, meeting Cane by the door. "Who'd've known?"

Walking out of the conference room together, the two exchanged not-as-awkward pleasantries. They even shared a laugh. It wasn't as if moments like this happened regularly around the office. Etta tried hard to ignore Agnes's insinuating glances toward them as they passed. But as far as she could tell, Cane didn't notice either Agnes's look or Etta's own reddening complexion.

"I'm gonna head to the breakroom and grab a cup of coffee if you're interested," Cane offered just before reaching Etta's cubicle, which sat directly across from the breakroom.

"Nah." She shook her head. "I'm not a fan of the stuff in there."

"Ah, a coffee snob," Cane quipped.

"Yeah, well…" Her voice trailed off. "Life's too short for shitty coffee."

"Touché," Cane conceded, heading into the breakroom and leaving Etta relatively light-headed, leaning against the opening of her cubicle. Agnes strutted by Etta on her way to the breakroom, humming what sounded like a slowed-down, mildly taunting version of *Pop Goes the Weasel*. Questionably embarrassed, Etta darted into her cubicle.

She sat in her spinning chair and pulled up her online Scrabble game, contemplating her next move. Her anonymous opponent dropped *candid* for ten points, and Etta let out a frustrated groan. The tiles on the animated board taunted her, pressuring her to come up with something brilliant. Something clever. Cautiously, she pulled the letters from her stand, playing *whisk* for fifteen points.

Relaxing into her office chair, Etta could see Cane pouring coffee into their mug. A smug smile spread across their face as she stared for a moment too long. Turning back to her screen, Etta's face fell. The letters K, E, T, C, H, I, N, and G sprouted off of her S, spelling out *sketching* for nineteen points and winning the game.

A message bubble popped up on the screen.

"rematch" the anonymous opponent propositioned without any punctuation or capitalization.

Etta stared at the pop-up thinking about the nerve this player must have. How lazy they must be to not capitalize the R or even push the two buttons needed to punctuate the one-word sentence with a question mark. But her desire to beat them took precedent, and she clicked on *Play Again* as spitefully as one could muster when pressing an animated button.

Crashing through her apartment door, Etta slid down to the floor and closed it behind her. The air from the ground faintly smelled of cat dander and Italian food, and she looked up at the kitchenette. Steam rose from two medium-sized pots on the stove and a salad bowl sat on the counter. Cleese pounced from the top of the refrigerator, squaring up and locking eyes with Etta. She glared back through her foggy glasses, catching her winded and startled breath.

"Rough day?" Sam chuckled, making his way out of the bathroom while toweling off his wet hair. "Tst—be nice," he muttered, scooting his foot in front of Cleese to deescalate his stance.

"No. Just strange… ish…" she replied before sticking her tongue out at Cleese and wiping off her glasses. Even through the blur, she knew Sam was rolling his eyes as he offered his hand. Yanking her off the floor, her roommate moved toward the stove to dump something into the boiling larger pot and stirred. "What's cooking?"

"Gnocchi," Sam answered, carefully watching the dumplings float to the surface. He lifted the wooden spoon to his lips, blowing on it before shoving one into his mouth. "Riley and I are staying in tonight. Are you?"

Etta slumped over to a stool after throwing her jacket on the back and rested her head on the counter. Cleese jumped up, plopping next to her face, his tail swatting her arms.

"Guess not," she replied, pushing the cat away and lifting her head. "I'll probably go into Amherst and go to The Attic."

"I'm not kicking you out, ya know. And you do realize Amherst is over a half hour away. Right?" Sam asked, walking over to the sink to wash the dirty dishes that had accumulated over the last few days. "It's a Wednesday night. Besides, what do you even do at The Attic?"

"I'm aware," Etta huffed. "And Dorian gives me coffee from a French press and then leaves me alone as I browse through the shelves. He's trying to restore some old literary magazine, so he doesn't mind me loitering. Secretly, I think he likes the company."

Sam threw the dish towel on top of Etta's head, a slightly concerned look on his face. "One, you don't need the caffeine. And two, you're drying. These dishes are yours too. I don't want Riley to know how slobbish we are yet."

Etta groaned. Dishes were her least favorite thing to do. Next to laundry. She slunk off her stool and dutifully stood next to her roommate.

"You're just like my mother," she muttered, grabbing a wet plate from the drying rack. "Actually, you're worse."

"Bullshit!" Sam guffawed, stacking another plate onto her pile. "I bet your mother doesn't let you get away with half of what I do!"

"Actually," Etta began, drying the dishes with a smile of gross satisfaction and lowering her voice to a fake whisper, "she lets me get away with more."

A loud, sarcastic sound erupted from Sam's mouth, all culminating in one syllable and startling Cleese off the counter. The sudden movement alarmed Etta, making her aware of Cleese's absence from her peripheral vision.

"That definitely explains a lot," Sam teased, rinsing off the last plate and stacking it. Etta neared the end of her pile while Sam squatted to the ground trying to coax Cleese back to his spot. "So, you never said. Why was your day 'strange-ish?'"

Drying the last plate, Etta hesitated to answer. She opened the cupboard door and put them away, carefully choosing her words.

"Okay, well…" She looked to her roommate whose face indicated he knew a rant was fast approaching.

"Please understand that when I say strange, I don't mean bizarre, or surreal, or weird. I mean atypical, or out of the ordinary, or—better yet—doesn't usually happen on a daily basis," Etta clarified, her hands emphasizing how important it was for Sam to understand. He laughed as he stood up from the floor and then leaned against the wall, trying to avoid hitting his head on the hanging pots and pans. "Okay?"

"My dear Odette," Sam teased. "I know you like words and their exact definitions and being precise. Like, that's your thing. But I think I get it."

"But do you?"

"Yes," he punctuated with a clap. "Now stop stalling."

Sighing, Etta closed the cabinet door and then dried off the edge of the counter before turning around to lean on it. Her head rolled to the back of her neck and then hung heavily in front of her before conceding.

"Fine. Okay. So, I've told you about my coworker with the *Top Gun* jacket. Right?" Etta asked almost timidly. The dawdling had nothing to do with Sam's—or even Cleese's idling—presence. Feelings outside of the hungry or tired category always posed a particular amount of discomfort, those Sam occasionally teased her for. So maybe Sam's presence contributed to the circle-talk a little bit.

"The one who cuffs their sleeves, wears motorcycle boots, and supposedly drinks more coffee than you do?" Sam asked.

"Yes. Exactly. Well, we talked today," she confessed. Her lower lip stung from pulling the dead skin away.

"Odette. My love. Work with me here." At face value, Sam's words sounded encouraging, but the impatience grew louder in his tone as it tended to do whenever he crowbarred anything out of her. "Do you mean like in passing or a full conversation?"

"Actually…" she began to answer, her voice dragging toward the end. "They helped me in Scrabble."

Sam's brow came together, his eyes shifting back and forth. Etta watched her roommate move toward the stove to spoon out the cooked gnocchi. He looked at her over his shoulder and passed her the full colander. Walking to the sink with the pasta water, Sam collected his words. "Is… that… all?"

Etta stepped out of the way as Sam drained all the water. The steam rose like a small mushroom cloud and wafted over her face, leaving it moist. Peeling away a piece of hair, Etta grabbed a napkin to wipe off her face before nodding in response.

The doorbell of the apartment buzzed, causing the pair to jump. Sam checked his phone, typed something out, and then dumped the drained gnocchi back into its original pot.

"There was joking involved, too," Etta quickly added, hoping Sam wouldn't think her interaction with Cane was incredibly insignificant. It wasn't significant by any means, but it wasn't insignificant either.

Sam turned to her with tight lips and an unsure expression on his face. His hand flew up to his chin as if thinking and then deeply sighed, his body and face relaxing. "Okay, Riley's downstairs. I'm gonna go let him in," Sam said.

As he made his way toward the door, he turned to face Etta with a quizzical expression. "Is Scrabble like foreplay for you or something?" he asked before quite literally shaking the thought out of his head. "You know what? Never mind. We'll discuss later."

Etta crept to her room, throwing her backpack onto the unmade bed. Meandering to her closet, she kicked her shoes into a basket and peeled off her work slacks before tossing them on the floor. She unbuttoned her shirt and turned to face her one-window bedroom with the floor lamp casting a warm light across the white walls, muting their brightness. Etta reached for the already once-worn jeans lying on the floor and grabbed a different shirt from her dresser.

She took a tally of all the items she would bring to The Attic. A book, maybe? There'd be books there, but Etta always liked to have one on hand. A sweatshirt, just in case. Of course, she'd bring her notebook. That wasn't a question, and it was already in her backpack. Her headphones, as The Attic often got unsettlingly quiet. And finally, her laptop to continue her Scrabbles games—especially against the player she named Grammatically Incorrect Rematch, or Gir for short.

Muffled laughter quickly approached the front door before Sam and an unknown voice she assumed to be Riley's entered and stood near the kitchen. Riley's voice was deep and warm, and the pair sounded happy like they were having a good time. Meaning she should probably collect her things faster so she could get out of their hair.

Throwing everything into her backpack, Etta made her way out of her bedroom. She tried to sneak away but nearly bumped into the tall stranger with reddish hair contrasting his dark complexion.

"Oh!" he said, clearly startled by the sudden appearance of a third body. "You must be Etta."

"Yeah. Odette, actually," she corrected hesitantly, her voice stammering. She wasn't sure why she told him her given name. It wasn't a formal setting. This was her own home, and he was a guest. But Etta brushed it off as nerves and was thankful Sam didn't witness her spasm.

"I'm Riley. It's nice to finally put a name to the face… I mean a face to the name." The stranger laughed, reaching out his hand. Clutching the strap of her backpack, Etta shyly offered her free hand. It was clear he wasn't aware of her internal faux pas.

Sam popped his head around the corner from the kitchen as Cleese sauntered into the living room from between his legs. The cat stopped short at the sight of Riley who quietly squatted down to his eye level.

"You have a cat!" Riley said in the soothing yet excited voice that people reserve just for babies and animals. "He's adorable!"

Etta looked over at Sam, who watched Riley offer a hand to the cat before softly grazing the top of his head. Cleese welcomed the interaction and settled at Riley's feet, allowing the stranger to continue the petting. Etta saw her roommate smile at the pair before catching her eye. She felt the blankness of her face before pulling her mouth into a grin. Smiling wider than her, Sam stepped into the living room.

"How are you getting to Amherst?" Sam asked, turning his attention to her as she shrugged in response. He laughed. "Would you like to borrow my car?"

"Yes, please," Etta replied almost too eagerly. "I'd really appreciate it."

"Quick question," Sam began, walking over to grab his keys. "Being from Joisey and all—do you even know how to pump gas?"

"First off, I have never, in my life, *ever* heard anyone authentically use that pronunciation," Etta asserted while watching Riley scoop up the cat and walk over to the couch. "Second, I've done it before."

"Awesome!" Sam blurted, ignoring the declaration entirely. "Then do you mind filling up the tank since you're going pretty far?"

She nodded again before taking the keys from Sam and heading toward the door. "Yeah, no problem. Thanks again," she said as she waved to the pair.

"It was nice meeting you!" Riley called after her.

"*Yallah*, please be careful!" Sam laughed.

Etta rolled her eyes as she left the apartment.

CHAPTER 4

———

Etta parked her roommate's car and speed-walked toward
The Attic, trying to minimize her time spent out in the cold.
The wooden sign swung by the glass front door like one above
an old pub. Dirty shades covered the front window and door
from the inside, accentuating the chipping dirty gold paint
that spelled "Dorian's Attic." Odette pulled the heavy door
and stepped inside.

The Attic was dark for a bookstore. The streetlights shining through the shades revealed an overwhelming haze of
dust looming overhead. Antique Tiffany lamps stood scattered throughout the store and cast light at the end of every
other bookshelf, each holding vintage and used books
donated from families of their deceased relatives or bought
by Dorian at both classy and storage-space auctions.

Walking deeper into the store, Etta spotted an empty Styrofoam cup sitting next to the register, tagged with a sticky
note. *Coffee prepared* was scratched out in Dorian's sharply
slanted handwriting. She walked behind the counter, hanging up her jacket in the giant armoire, and then grabbed the

French Press to pour herself a cup. Resting the cup on her lips, Etta let the last bit of frostbite melt away.

"Etta?" a voice called from over the upstairs railing. "Etta! I have something to show you!"

A middle-aged man carrying a comically large book descended the metal, spiral staircase. His glasses precariously hung on the tip of his nose, and an unlit cigarette sat tucked behind his ear. His salt-and-pepper hair was all disheveled, clearly from repeatedly trying to push it out of his eyes while hovering over this giant, aged book for what was—knowing Dorian—most likely hours.

"Quick!" he continued, pointing behind the counter. "Grab the cloth from the top drawer. I don't want the counter to scratch the cover! It is in an unbelievably marvelous shape considering how old it is. Well, come on!"

Etta pulled open the drawer and found a thin, white towel sitting in an open box. Dorian cradled the book in one arm while frantically pointing toward the still-open drawer.

"Lay it out. Hell if I'm the one who ruins this damn book beyond repair. It is far too fantastic!"

She spread out the cloth—although it felt more like an overused kitchen towel—across the counter as instructed. Etta had never been on the receiving end of a cross Dorian. But since witnessing it, she knew it was best to follow his particularity. Laying the book down as gently as he could, Dorian slowly opened the cover. Pointing to the title page art, he then grabbed Etta's hand, running her fingers over the illustration.

"Do you feel how it's raised? Yeah? Do you feel it? It's from the printing press. Published long before laser printers. And take a look at this!" he nearly screamed, turning the pages painfully slowly, practically one by one until he was about a quarter-way into the book. This side of Dorian rarely made an appearance, but Etta loved seeing it. She beamed at the fascination pouring from his expression. "Do you see the language? Do you see the words?"

Etta brought her face closer to the pages. "When's this from? The seventeenth century?"

"Careful! Don't breathe too heavily near it—the moisture from your breath can do damage." Etta backed up a little as Dorian shoved the magnifying glass from his back pocket into her hand. "Even earlier! It's written in Middle English, so probably somewhere from the 1450s to the early 1500s. But look at this word specifically: *lyfdæg.*" Dorian excitedly pointed his finger to the middle of the page, his sallow-skinned hand starkly white compared to the aged, yellow page. "What do you think this would translate to today?"

She took a moment to study the word. Knowing the book was in Middle English—probably the West Saxon dialect, Etta noted, as the spelling was considerably consistent compared to other works Dorian had shown her in the past—Etta was able to recognize more characteristics to come to an answer. She began sounding the words out under her breath.

"I mean, *lyf* is obviously going to translate to *life*—"

"Right at the start of the Great Vowel Shift!" Dorian exclaimed

Etta smiled at the interjection and continued on. "*Dæg* sounds like *tag* which is German for *day*, right? So *life-day?* Like 'a day in the life?'"

"Close!" Dorian gestured his hands for Etta to continue.

"But that doesn't make a lot of sense because it's probably not a literal translation. So probably more like the essence of a life-day, so... *Day... Night?* But that doesn't make any more sense than..." Dorian excitedly shook his head, encouraging her away from that train of thought. "I mean, *Day* is a measure of *time*. Right? So... *Time? Life? Life-ti... Lifetime!* It's *lifetime!*" Etta yelled as Dorian clapped his hands together.

"The history of language is so damn cool," Dorian raved, continuing on about the book and its words. Etta nodded along to Dorian's impassioned lecture, reaching for her coffee cup.

"What do you think you're doing?" Dorian shouted, stopping mid-sentence and startling her. Etta felt her eyes widen as she waited for him to continue. "Do you know what could happen if even a drop of that fell on this book? History. Defiled! All because you were careless with your cup of coffee."

Etta quickly but carefully moved the coffee to the table behind them, her heart pattering like it did on her late mornings when she needed to run to work.

"Dorian, I'm so sorry," she fawned. "I completely forgot! I wasn't thinking. I'm sorry."

Dorian watched her for a moment and then calmed himself. "It's okay," he replied, lowering his voice. "Just be more careful next time."

"Absolutely," Etta promised. While her frenzied heart stabilized, the guilt settled, weighing down her body. "And thank you again for the coffee. I always appreciate it."

"Sensitive subject," Dorian said, gingerly closing the book and cradling it back to his office.

Paralyzed for a moment, Etta waited for the last of Dorian's footsteps at the top of the stairs. Then she folded the towel and stored it back in the drawer.

She reached under the counter, feeling around for Dorian's newest *Oxford English Dictionary* edition she'd stashed a month earlier. Throwing her bag over her shoulder and tucking the dictionary under her arm, Etta ambled through the stacks to her favorite spot. Shelves stuffed with books spread from front to back. Some were leatherbound while others still owned their jackets, and a few had embossment that still gleamed when it caught the light. All were yellowed from age.

Etta found a small table near the back of the store where she knew she wouldn't be disturbed. Not that anyone came into the store to be bothersome anyway. Dorian had a knack for scaring customers away by following them and whispering mordant comments in their ears. It was a wonder he was able to stay in business for so long. But Etta always assumed he'd inherited a substantial amount of money within his *lyfdæg* and used that to keep the store afloat. She couldn't recall Dorian mentioning any other family, so it wasn't an impossibility.

Pulling out her laptop and notebook from her backpack, Etta sprawled them across the tiny surface, taking up more space than necessary. She flicked the switch of the table lamp, and a cone of light pierced through the surrounding darkness, reminding her of a spotlight. Etta half-expected to see a tiny man with a cane—dressed in a black suit and bowler hat—appear beneath the light shouting "*Willkommen! And bienvenue.* Welcome!" But the show was clearly delayed, and the rumble of the imaginary audience grew louder, the sound threatening to lodge and expand itself deep in Etta's ear canal. She quickly unraveled her headphones before it got the chance to settle.

Grabbing the book from her bag, she placed the spine down on the table and the page fell open to where she left off. A few words were underlined in red and numbered, correlating to the extensive etymological map documented in her notebook. The last highlighted word on the page was *ritzy* and marked as 223 in the margins. Etta cross-checked it to the entry in her notebook.

Ritzy—first used in the early 1920s—meaning stylish/classy while simultaneously ostentatious and gaudy, became a shorthand version of the adjective Ritzian, a word to describe the luxurious characteristics found in the Hôtel Ritz of Paris and The Ritz Hotel of London—both named after the famous Swiss hotelier César Ritz, nicknamed "king of hoteliers, and hotelier to kings."

Etta continued reading, making sure to underline the words she found interesting, assigning them a number, and then jotting it down in her notebook. Then she'd look up their definitions in the *Oxford English Dictionary* to then later track and record their etymological paths both from memory and online research.

She picked up her pen and began listing out more:

224. Nickname—a (usually familiar or humorous) name given to a person, place, etc., as a supposedly appropriate replacement for or addition to the proper name—a misdivision of the word ekename from the mid-1500s, deriving from the Old English phrase an eke name, which literally translates to "an additional name."

225. Acknowledge—to accept authority, validity, or legitimacy of—a blend of the Middle English acknow (from the Old English word oncnawan—to understand or recognize) and the Middle English knowlechen (to admit).

- *In the merger, a -c- slipped in, so that when the kn- became a simple "n" sound, the -c- stepped up to preserve the "kn-" sound.*
- *The silent -k- fell into colloquial somewhere during the seventeenth and eighteenth centuries.*

226. 227. 228. And so on until Etta lost track of time.

An unexpected hand rested on Etta's shoulder, causing her to jump. The jarring grind of the chair against the floor hacked through the dead air. She turned around, wired from the adrenaline rush and caffeine. Glasses resting on the top of his head, Dorian offered a detached smile and rubbed his eyes. "It's nearly eleven. I need to start closing up and heading home."

"Oh…" Etta turned to face her belongings spread out in front of her. "Okay. Just give me a minute to pack everything up, and I'll be out of your hair."

"No problem." Dorian yawned, adjusting his glasses back over his eyes and walking away. "Take your time. I'm going to clear everyone else out."

Etta looked over her shoulder to the empty store. Regardless, she collected her things and headed toward the front where Dorian stood, mindlessly playing with the register. She tossed her empty cup into the trashcan and opened the armoire to grab her jacket. As she watched Dorian repeatedly eject the register drawer and push it back in, Etta studied his face, looking for any sign that he was still upset over the earlier coffee non-incident.

"So… How's everything? Like life and stuff?" Etta asked, her voice cracking a little bit.

Dorian turned around, leaning up against the counter, no clues given. "It's comfortable. It's just me and my store and my auctions and my books."

"Right," Etta offered, pulling on her jacket and throwing her backpack over her shoulders. She figured his answer would amount to as much. Dorian patted the pockets of his jeans before pulling out a pack of cigarettes and a lighter. "Thank you again for the coffee."

"Mm-hmm." Dorian neutrally waved as she left The Attic.

Walking toward Sam's car, Etta continued fretting over whether Dorian was still upset. He didn't seem any different than usual, but she hoped he knew she was genuinely sorry. Since leaving her hometown, The Attic had become an escapist sanctuary for Etta. After moving in followed by too many consecutive weekends sans plans, Etta promptly grew stir crazy. She'd hopelessly reached out to Emily, a college friend living in Amherst, who canceled right as Etta's bus pulled into town. Not wanting to waste the trip, Etta searched for the one public place where she didn't mind being alone—a bookshop. Etta didn't know what she'd do if she was no longer welcome at The Attic.

Hopping in the car, Etta inspected Sam's CD collection, eventually settling on a playlist from her phone. She threw it in the cupholder acting as a makeshift amp and headed home. The caffeine from her earlier coffee exaggerated her pulse as it mimicked the throbbing bass of the Rilo Kiley song.

The flashes of passing street lamps reminded Etta of the midnight drives she would take with Emily and their other friends. After hours of chugging cafeteria coffee and studying in the library, the group would become antsy. Unable to close their eyes, they'd pile into a too-small car, sitting on each other's laps to compensate for the lack of space. They'd cruise the wooded neighborhoods, letting the sticky summer night breeze through the open windows. When their legs grew stiff, they'd stop at the local parks. Lying in the fields, staring at the stars, the friends created their own constellations, imagining the correlating myths. The only stars Etta gazed at now were on her wintry walks home from work.

Before she knew it, Etta was pulling into Sam's parking spot. She snatched her phone, turned off the music, and collected the rest of her things. As she walked up the stairs toward her apartment, she felt the fog of a caffeine crash looming and gratitude for her nearby bed as her brain puttered like a backfiring car. Stepping inside, she threw her keys next to the fountain and noticed a single light diffusing across the kitchenette. Her eyes adjusted to the new lighting, and Etta briefly spotted Sam's boxers peeking from behind the open refrigerator door before they disappeared and were replaced by his head.

"Riley's asleep," he hushed. "But I got hungry."

"Good date?" Etta cheekily asked, watching her roommate pick at leftover salad with his fingers. Sam wiggled his shoulders and pursed his lips, smiling like he had a secret.

"He likes my cooking," he tittered and then continued gushing about his date with Riley, reminiscing about their comfortable night in. After Etta left, Sam served dinner and they cozied on the couch while watching *The Meaning of Life* as Cleese curled up at Riley's feet.

"That sounds nice," Etta replied, her ears popping as she held back a yawn.

"And your night?" Sam resealed the leftovers before throwing them back into the fridge.

"Mostly quiet. I got yelled at a little because I almost spilled coffee on this super old book Dorian showed me," Etta began, her tired eyes straining at the combined tension of remembering the incident and her growing fatigue. Sam's hand flipped out and over toward her, his head twitching as if gently electrocuted. She knew from past run-ins with the gesture that he was prompting her to continue. "I mean, he yelled before my hand even touched the cup. But I get it. That book was literally from the late fifteenth century, and we both know I'm a spaz…"

Clicking his tongue, Sam rolled his eyes.

"What?" she asked, surprised by his reaction.

"I just think it's sad," he began, heading toward his room. "The man sounds like a hermit. And if he's as reclusive as I think he is, he shouldn't be raising his voice at what sounds like his only friend. Especially when you did nothing wrong."

Etta's head followed her roommate as she stood silently. She never thought of Dorian as a hermit, but it wasn't a leap to assume so. On top of never speaking about anyone—as far as she knew—Etta was the only regular at The Attic and the only customer Dorian exchanged civil dialogue with.

"It's just a sad existence," Sam continued, biting his lip. "To have nothing or no one, and to be stuck with a bookstore he inherited from who-the-hell-knows."

"He does seem to like it," Etta tried rebutting.

"Does he?" Sam challenged, stopping outside his bedroom door. "I don't think you've once described the man in a good mood after coming home from that place. He's always shouting at someone or holed up in his office. That's what isolation does to people."

Etta's eyes shifted back and forth, reflecting on her own day-to-day and lack of social circle. Although not in the habit of snapping at people, when Etta wasn't at work, she holed herself up in a coffee shop, The Attic, or their apartment. Her eyebrows came together in worry as she looked up at her roommate who followed her train of thought and interjected.

"You should come out with me more instead of spending all your time at that store. It's not like you buy books from there that often anyway," Sam backpedaled. "You've been here for almost a year at this point. It's time to meet some new people!"

"I guess," Etta muttered.

"Great!" Sam softly clapped. "You can come out with Riley and me tomorrow night. It'll be good for you! Besides, you don't really want to spend the rest of your days in the back of a bookstore that's not even yours."

Sam cupped Etta's shoulder, smiled, and then softly said goodnight before disappearing behind his bedroom door. His words hollowed a cavern in Etta's chest. Standing in her living room, now alone in more ways than one, Etta wondered what Dorian was like outside of The Attic. Was he just as surly in private? And was he always like that? Was a lifetime of alienation—chosen or not—the cause of Dorian's distemper? Were hermits born or created? If Etta didn't find a connection, was that her future?

Etta never considered the similarities between her and Dorian before. She enjoyed his company because of his knowledge of books and the history of the English language. They'd get lost for hours silently looking through books for words they didn't recognize and then scurry to the *Oxford English Dictionary* to find their relatives. But outside of that, Etta couldn't draw many other parallels without some serious stretch. And so long as that remained true, she told herself not to worry. It was too late for an identity crisis, and she didn't have the energy to sort anything out.

CHAPTER 5

———

Etta hid her face in the crook of her elbow. The lack of sleep bloated her under-eyes and her lunch bloated her stomach. Groaning, she told herself to rally through the last three hours of the work*daeg*. However, remembering she had 19,864 words left made it all the more difficult to open her eyes. At least she was over halfway through.

Swiveling side to side in her chair, Etta hoped Riley had as great of a time as Sam did. Riley seemed excited when he saw Cleese, and the two were getting along really well before she left for Amherst—Sam and Riley, but Cleese and Riley too, which she guessed was important considering how important Cleese was to Sam. Everything seemed easy for them in that moment. A lot easier than Sam and Jesse had it. Or even Sam and Cameron, or Sam and Lane, or Sam and Avery, or Sam and Drew. Or Sam and Alina, which was just all sorts of wrong.

Staring at her computer screen, Etta tried thinking of a way to shorten the definition of *migrant*. "A bird or animal that moves from one area to another at different times of the year" seemed pretty short and accurate enough. Besides, it was still far less interesting than the idea that the word *migrant* comes from the Latin verb *migrāre* meaning "to remove, to depart, to move from one place to another" and its earliest recording of being used as a noun and in regard to birds was in 1672 by Sir Thomas Browne in his *A Letter to a Friend.*

But Etta thought about how *migrant* had a richer history than just talking about birds. Like how during the Great Depression, groups of people labeled Migrants drifted along Route 66 in search of jobs—any job—to feed themselves or their families. During the Dust Bowl, Californians took to calling any and all migrant workers *Oakies*—inferring most of these people were coming from Oklahoma. But in doing so, Californians drew attention to the suffering working class, influencing John Steinbeck to write one of his most famous novels, *The Grapes of Wrath*, and causing the government to take serious action in helping its people, thus instating The New Deal.

Albeit a self-oversimplification, Etta could relate. Although eighty years too late, she too was a Migrant. She moved from Jersey to Northampton in search of a life—any life—anything she could bring back home and say, "See, everyone, I can survive."

Etta was the last of her friends back at home. Everyone else had finished college, found important jobs they were passionate about, and most found a partner to settle in with. They were so quick to take what was left of their childhood and pack it away, deep in their forget-me-not trunks at the backs of their closets. Etta had one too, but compared to her friends, she took hers out to reflect back more than they did. So while they were out finding new lives, Etta sat in her attic, alone, surrounded by the old.

Northampton was an impulse—one fueled by unrest and unfounded guilt triggered by a prolonged stint of isolation after her last college friend received their out-of-state job offer. After too many years of failing to achieve normalcy, Etta panicked upon realizing it no longer existed. Everything she once knew as routine slowly dissolved. Like a handful of sugar in the rain, the confection falling through her fingers felt pleasant. But as soon as the last of it slipped away, Etta was left with nothing more than a crystallizing hand becoming harder to move the longer she let it be.

Worried the rest of her would become solid, Etta began to move. Just like the Oakies, she knew opportunity lay elsewhere. So she took to the modern-day equivalent of the wild, wild West—the world wide web—in search of anything that could get her out of the attic. And out of uncertainty and desperation, she applied to the only company whose name brought her any sort of feeling—the rhyming pun didn't hurt.

Etta put *migrant* aside and pulled up her online Scrabble game. She could tell Denise was suffering. *Hat* lay alongside Etta's *tennis*, and *go* feebly stretched down out of *oxygen*. The end was near. It was painfully obvious who the victor would be.

"How much longer until the baby arrives?" Etta heard Agnes's accent travel from down the hall.

"Jenny has about six more weeks until her due date," Valeska answered as she and Agnes neared the breakroom. Etta closed out of Scrabble and pulled work back up, afraid of being caught slacking. She swiveled in her chair and watched as Valeska and Agnes sat around the table—Agnes with her yogurt and Valeska with her mug.

"This is all so exciting!" Agnes continued, her voice trilling. "I remember when my oldest, Markus, was born. Bradley and I were so excited; we just couldn't wait. You must be so excited! How excited are you?"

"We're pretty excited." Valeska laughed out of pure friendliness. "Mostly, I just can't wait for Jenny's heartburn to go away. There's been nothing but kale, grilled chicken, and lentils around the house for months now. I'm dying for her lamb vindaloo!"

Etta's cubicle was in a prime location for eavesdropping. For the few months she'd been at Brain Train, she couldn't help but listen in—not because what her coworkers were discussing was so titillating, but because she was perfectly within listening distance.

Listening in was inherently in Etta's nature. She'd mastered the skill as a young child. As she played pretend in closets searching for Narnia or whole other worlds, Etta quickly picked up on her ability to snoop. Blending into the background or becoming a part of the tableau became her specialty, and with it came unforeseen benefits. She'd learned of the best family gossip this way—like her cousin's graduation Botox, her other cousin's affair with his boss, and her grandmother's cancer.

Etta disclosed this habit once to Sam, who responded with a snarky comment. And when she tried to defend herself, he rebutted with the unfairness of catching people at their most vulnerable without reciprocation or even consent. But you could learn a lot about character through what people spoke of behind closed doors.

"I'm not really one for ethnic food," Agnes continued, "but that I might like. Back when I was younger, my *oma* would go to the local butcher and make a big lamb for every Easter. Lamb was always my favorite."

"And garlic naan!" Valeska continued, sort of ignoring Agnes. "Oh god, I would kill for her garlic naan…"

Etta sat in her chair and thought of an excuse to join them. She completely despised the coffee in the breakroom—a well-known fact around the office—leaving that excuse null and void. And she'd already eaten her leftovers from the fridge, so that was lost as well. Etta stood up anyway and walked across the tiny hall.

"Hi." She smiled as she waved to her coworkers. They returned her smile brightly.

"What're you doing here?" Agnes theatrically asked. "You're almost never in the breakroom!"

Etta quickly pulled a dollar out of her cardigan pocket and walked closer to the vending machine. "Just getting a snack," she replied, remembering how heavy her stomach felt from lunch.

"Feeling peckish?" Agnes's voice neared a whisper.

Self-consciously, Etta nodded her head and turned to face the myriad of options in front of her, none of which she wanted or felt she had the actual ability to consume.

Staring at the machine, she chose a letter and a number at random, ending up with M&Ms—unfortunately not the peanut or the pretzel kind. She would've graciously accepted those instead of submitting to plain milk chocolate. Even if they did melt in your mouth, and not your hand—which Etta discovered at a very young age was a lie if you held on to them for long enough.

"Anyway!" Agnes continued, turning her attention back to Valeska. "Is it a boy or a girl?"

"We don't know. We want it to be a surprise."

"Oh! How fun! Well, which do you want more?" Agnes prodded.

"I—"

"Yes, you'll be happy with either, and yes, you just want the baby to be healthy! But between us girls, which would you prefer?"

Etta leaned up against the vending machine and really held back from rolling her eyes. No matter how many times she tried, she would just never be a baby person. But she'd committed to coming into the breakroom. This was the choice she'd made—unlike the M&M-not-choice—and she was going to stick it out. Besides, it was a much better option than actually going back to work or watching Denise endure the torture of losing another round of Scrabble. And if she went home and told Sam all about how social she was at work, maybe he wouldn't force her to go out tonight.

"I honestly don't care," Valeska responded earnestly. "And neither does Jenny. The nursery is light green because it's supposed to be a popular, soft, gender-neutral color."

"Yeah," Etta offered, opening her bag of unwanted, hard-shell candy. As she reached into the bag for her first piece, Cane walked in, empty mug in hand, casually smiled at her, and headed over to the coffee maker. Her voice was soft. "I heard that somewhere."

"How nice!" Agnes said, her voice growing louder and her accent getting thicker out of pure excitement, as she failed to acknowledge the extra body in the room. "Have you thought of any names?"

Valeska looked at Etta, shared a smile of camaraderie, and then looked back toward Agnes. "Jenny and I both really like the name Devin for either."

"I really like that," Etta responded as the wheels in her head started turning. She vaguely remembered looking up a similar word recently, and a word tree appeared in her head. Behind her eyes, she saw the name "Devin" as a bud sprouting from a twig.

"Thank you." Valeska smiled widely and opened her mouth to say something.

"That's an Old French word for *divine*," Etta shared as "Devin" sprouted from the "divine." As it further stretched in her mind, the shoots of similar words grew sturdier toward full branches connecting to the fat trunk.

"Well, it really translates into Modern English as *soothsayer*, but *devin*—the French word—comes from the Latin word *divinus*—which means ecclesiastic or of a god," she continued. "The *div-* part of *divinus* is from the Latin base for 'god,' the *-in* literally means 'pertaining to,' and *-us* is the shortened version of *o-u-s* meaning 'full of.' So *divinus* literally translates to 'full of god'—which then relates to the *deus*, which, as you can probably tell, sounds very much like Zeus, which isn't a coincidence by any means."

In the small breakroom, Etta's imaginary tree began to grow until it became a part of the foreground. The coworkers in front of her felt distant as if they stood on the other side of the tree. And as their eyes only looked toward her and not the natural wonder flourishing between them, Etta continued to describe its majesty.

"It's also closely related to the Sanskrit root word *deva-*." Etta followed the tree in her mind like a skittering squirrel. "Or *devi-* in the feminine term—and also to the Persian root word *div-*, which unfortunately has the negative connotation in the Avestan language of supernatural being with unfavorable characteristics. But the connotation of the Avestan language doesn't really apply in this case since modern-day concepts of divinity mainly express goodness, justice, and beauty, which I'm sure is what you and Jenny were really trying to get at."

Both Valeska and Agnes looked at Etta for a moment, their mouths slightly ajar. Cane turned their head toward Etta with a receptive smile as they reached into the refrigerator for the milk. Etta could feel her body stiffen and cheeks warm as the tree grew so tall it split in half with a deafening crack.

"Yeah," Valeska pleasantly laughed. "Jenny and I read the name in a book and really liked that. The *divine* part, at least. Our book of names wasn't as detailed as you just were, though."

"How do you know this?" Agnes asked, feigning intrigue.

Etta leaned harder into the vending machine, her embarrassment rising.

"Did you take Latin in college or something?" Cane contributed after Etta's lack of response lasted a second too long.

She took a deep breath and managed not to stammer out, "No. I took a phonetics course and a class on language histories. But basically, I just really like etymology. I do a lot of research on my own time."

"How neat," Agnes said, shoving a spoonful of yogurt into her mouth.

Etta placed an M&M between her teeth, letting her eyes fall to the side. Agnes continued asking Valeska baby questions as Etta stewed in discomfort. The broken word tree was suddenly experiencing a termite and ant situation as she watched it being devoured from the inside before rotting into the cold breakroom tiles.

"So," Cane began, breaking Etta's faraway stare. "Words, huh?"

Etta shrugged and nodded, unsure of how else to respond when dismissal still hung heavy.

"Sounds like you found a fitting job for your passions." They laughed. "Not many people get paid for their special interests."

Ready to rebut, her eyes hastily shot up at her coworker who stood with a shit-eating, teasing grin on their face. Etta softened, her insecurity and embarrassment melting away. "Calling our work a special interest is a bit of a stretch. Don't ya think?"

Cane nodded and smiled, allowing Etta to feel comfortable enough to continue. "What about you?" she asked.

"Simply put, old books," Cane answered. "Bonus points if they have any sort of surreal history attached to them."

"Like what?" Etta prompted.

"Well," they continued, "I know of this book of allegories where each story invokes very specific sensations and feelings. And the cool part of this book is that apparently it's haunted or cursed or something and the reader starts to see things. Like their reality distorts and bends to align with the page."

"Distort reality?" Etta replied, the tree rot slowly falling away. "How? What does that mean?"

Cane shrugged. "No clue. But I'm curious nonetheless."

Etta popped a blue M&M into her mouth and nodded along, wondering if Dorian had ever heard of the book or knew its title. "Yeah, same. What's it called?"

Cane paused, looking down at their cup of shitty breakroom coffee. Etta was both amazed and grateful they were good at making conversation. "I actually can't remember. Someone told me about it a long time ago—or maybe I read about it somewhere—and I've been looking ever since, which proves to be sorta difficult when you can't remember the name."

"What a shame," Agnes said. Etta was uncertain if she was responding to Cane or Valeska.

"I can't remember where I found out about it. I just know it's out there, whether cursed or not," Cane lamented with a laugh. "But I would love to get my hands on it."

"You two should make an agreement," Agnes butted in, her face growing mischievous. "If either of you finds the book, you should share it with the other."

Cane looked over at Etta and smiled. "That is definitely something I can agree to."

"Same. I'll be on the lookout," Etta agreed, pouring a few M&Ms into her hand. As she headed back toward her cubicle, she internally congratulated herself on a successful breakroom interaction. Sam would be proud.

CHAPTER 6

———

Etta felt like a child dragged somewhere she didn't want to go. Sitting in the backseat of Sam's car, she sulked while Riley cackled in the passenger seat to something Sam said. Etta didn't catch it. As they passed under a streetlight, the raindrops raced one another down the window, and Etta sighed when hers didn't win. Had her evening not been seized by her roommate and his lover, Etta would've been at The Attic, asking Dorian question after question about Cane's book. Where did it come from? Who wrote it? Was it actually enchanted? What was it called?

They pulled up to the bar, an old, converted theater. The marquee listed different theme nights, drag shows, and events while rainbow flags and neon signs adorned the windows. Climbing out of the car, Etta heard the bass of the music coming from inside. With a dramatic sigh, she prepped herself to be deaf for the night.

"Miss Odette, perk up," Riley said, walking up from behind and wrapping his arm around her shoulders. Sam followed suit, playfully jostling her.

"This place is great—you're gonna love it," Sam began. "All of our friends go here, and it's where we met. They play fun music and the drinks aren't as expensive as the other places around. But you're sure to meet someone here!"

Etta held back an eyeroll. She didn't care to "meet" anybody. People were disappointing. Particularly new ones. She despised getting to know people, even back home. The small talk, the "what do you do," and the "where are you from" annoyed her. And it never took long for the new acquaintance to stop being on their best behavior, especially when alcohol was involved. But Sam was insistent, and Etta liked Sam, so she smiled back.

The bouncer recognized Riley and waved them in without checking their IDs. The atrium of the old theater was astronomically louder than what the outside insinuated. It had been converted into a dimly lit lounge area, and posters from the plays of yore adorned the walls. Large leather couches and armchairs occupied by couples in search of quieter moments clustered in the corners. Three sets of ornate, double doors separated the actual bar from the lounge. Every time they swung open, the bumping music pierced through Etta's ears—making her wish she had earplugs.

Etta and the boys handed their coats to the petite, crop-top-clad person working the coat-check room and then headed deeper inside. Spotting a table of their friends, Sam and Riley grabbed Etta by the hands and then dragged her through the crowd.

Awed by the room, Etta looked around. The orchestra seating was torn out of the retired theater and smoothed out into a dance floor. On the stage stood the DJ and her posse—a myriad of colorful characters, each one more out there than the next. Above, in the mezzanine, Etta spotted tables surrounded by bachelorette parties throwing shots, regulars judging the people below, and an out-of-place older couple.

One by one, Riley's friends scream-introduced themselves. She thought she made out their names over the music but wasn't entirely sure. What would it matter anyway? What was the likelihood of her speaking to any of these people after the night was over?

"I'm gonna grab a drink," Sam screamed to Etta. "What do you want?"

"Water," she yelled back.

"Great! Tequila shots it is!"

Before she could interject, Sam sprinted toward the bar.

One of Riley's friends—Etta believed her name was Claire. Or Blair. Or maybe Flair—who could actually tell over this music?—caught her eye and smiled. Her hair was slicked back in a tight bun, and the sheer top under her blazer made her look like she knew she was going out after a very important business meeting. Claire made her way around the group toward Etta.

"Isn't Riley great?" she said, leaning into Etta so she could hear.

Etta reciprocated. "Seems so—I don't know him that well yet."

"Give it time," Claire continued. "You'll come to love him."

Etta nodded, grabbing the shot offered by Sam and quickly downing it. But then came the what-do-you-dos. "I'm a copywriter."

"Oh, shit—that's awesome! Who do you write for?"

"A tutoring blog—I work on vocabulary flashcards." Claire nodded her head politely, taking a big swig from her glass. "What about you?"

"I'm a brand manager for a vegan co-op in Springfield. We're working on a city-wide campaign educating the public on the ecological and ethical benefits of circular consumption," Claire explained. "But I'm hoping this just becomes a stepping stone to something bigger. I'm really looking to consult for larger companies, potentially conglomerates. Any and all hope for a safe, healthy future relies on their cooperation." Etta felt herself becoming a part of the background. It came too easily when confronted with a talker. As her brain turned off, her instincts kicked in. The slow nodding. The subtle raising of the feigned-interest eyebrows. The mirroring of Claire's stance. These talents weren't dissimilar to her eavesdropping skills. Etta realized early on that polite conversation was inevitable. But while your chatting partner did expect you to respond, half the time, they didn't want you to contribute. So Etta learned the subconscious cadence of speech and the proper rhythm of head nods, the correct pitch of mm-hmms, and which beat to interject with a leading question. She was well-practiced.

The more difficult task, however, was avoiding comparisons. Claire's résumé—of which it seemed she'd never shut up about—was impressive. Whereas Etta's was inconsistent at best. Claire knew Big Shots, Trustfund Kids, and Influencers—although they were often one and the same, Claire explained. Etta barely knew Agnes, Terach, and Denise, and she'd worked with them for almost a year. But Etta was comfortable with Brain Train, her *Buffy* reruns, and Saturdays at The Attic. Etta was uncomfortable with eardrum-perforating bass kicks, strobe lights, and packs of people purposely neglecting the personal spaces of perfect strangers.

A strange hand wrapped around her wrist, breaking her concentration. Becoming instantly angry with a stranger's audacity to touch her, she turned to give them a piece of her mind. But outrage turned to pleasant surprise when Cane stood in front of her. Etta knew her voice was no match for the blaring music, so instead of saying hi, her hand shot up in a bewildered wave. Cane chuckled to themself, leaning in toward Etta's ear.

"Do you need a drink?" their shout sounded just under a regular speaking volume. After Cane pulled back to see her response, Etta theatrically nodded and laughed. Moving their grip from Etta's wrist to her hand, Cane led her to the bar. The mere touch rippled shockwaves through her pulse with the beat of the bass, disorienting her headspace.

Cane made a beeline to a single open stool and pulled it out. They gestured for Etta to take a seat and then leaned over to catch the bartender's attention. The leather of their jacket brushed against Etta's bare arm. Her skin buzzed. Or maybe it was the tequila shot. Cane looked back at Etta, sign-asking for her drink order, and then relayed the message to the bartender.

Drinks appeared in front of them and they slowly sipped. Now was Etta's chance. Although she knew Cane didn't have much more information about this mysterious book, she could still tell them about The Attic and Dorian and how he was probably their best bet in finding the thing. Each tried speaking or asking questions, but the blaring music made it impossible.

Cane took out their phone, beginning to text. Assuming they were losing interest, Etta felt dejected and cast her eyes across the bar, spotting Sam and Riley in an intimate dance circle. Cane tapped Etta's shoulder, showing her their phone screen. Their notes app was pulled up and read, *Want to get out of here? I can give you a ride home?*

She nodded, sent a quick text to Sam, and then followed Cane out the double doors and into the lounge. The stark noise difference felt like a massive bubble lodging itself deep in the ear canal. Getting in the coat check line, Etta massaged behind her ears to relieve the pressure with minimal success.

"So, you don't talk a lot at work," Cane began, sounding almost like they were underwater. Heat rose to Etta's cheeks. Being perceived was not something she was used to, especially as a self-proclaimed wallflower.

"There literally isn't a statement I hate more," she joked.

"Hasn't anyone ever explained to you that quiet folks don't like being identified as such?"

"Quiet people don't usually respond," Cane smugly replied, handing Etta her jacket. She held back a smile, and they continued on. "I guess it can be difficult to throw yourself into conversation as the new person. Huh? Pre-established work relationships and all. But you made some moves today!"

"Was it a move?" Etta interjected. "I felt it was more of a rejected info-dump, but I guess."

"Rejected by who?"

"Well, Agnes—"

"Who cares what Agnes thinks? She's like eighty years old!"

"Well, that's rude," Etta laughed. "Agnes is a sweet lady."

"A sweet lady who has some pretty outdated opinions she often imposes on others. I've been ignoring her for almost two years now—highly recommend."

The crisp, night air felt fresh against her sweaty, reddened cheek as she and Cane headed toward the car. As they piled in, Etta got a direct view of Cane's jacket and its other patches. The biggest was round and patriotically colored. Embroidered in large white letters, the patch read *Top Gun*, framed by a plane and a star.

Her head and eyes completely glued to Cane's shoulder, Etta could see their head turned toward her through her periphery.

Keeping her head completely still, Etta shifted her eyes to meet Cane's and responded with a bemused, apologetic smirk.

"It was my dad's," Cane answered without prompt. "He was a CSO for the Air National Guard. We bounced around a lot when I was a kid—Texas, Nevada, Wyoming—ya know, typical Army brat stuff."

Etta felt her face soften as she understood the jacket was the real deal and not just fan merch. "That's very sweet," she began, becoming endeared. "But is he even allowed to give it to you? Like, isn't that all a big deal?"

"I don't think he cares all that much," Cane laughed. "Ya know, being dead and all."

Etta's hands shot up to her face, covering her mouth. "Oh my god. I'm. So. Sorry." She wished she could catch her spoken words and shove them back down her throat. Or tie them around her waist and sink to the bottom of a murky lake where the freezing water would swallow her shame. Mortification had never felt so heavy.

But a bubbly laugh followed by a comforting hand on her knee brought Etta back to the surface. Her face still in her hands, Etta turned toward Cane, who was smiling with their eyes closed and shaking their head.

"It's really okay. He passed a long time ago. Like lots of dead-dad jokes among me and my sisters a long time ago. Like, Mom even gets in on the jokes, so it's totally fine."

No longer at the forefront of her brain, Etta became distracted by Cane's hand on her knee. Finding words difficult to string together, Etta stumbled through a half-assed, "Sisters, huh?" eliciting more lilting laughter from Cane.

"Yeah, two—Minnie and Sue. They're older, have kids of their own, and spend all their Sundays at Mom's for dinner. Leaving me off the hook to go about doing whatever I want."

"And that's working at Brain Train?" Etta teased, allowing herself to lighten up.

Cane snorted, placing their hand back on the steering wheel for a sharp turn. "Hell, no. This just pays the bills. Plus leaves me with some extra travel money. Did you know there's more out there than the five feet of snow blocking my door a few weeks ago?"

"Surprisingly, I did," she mocked.

Etta heard her phone *ding*. Pulling it out of her coat pocket, the notification bar read *have fun with army jacket—love Sam + Riley*. She let the phone fall into her lap, looked beyond the dashboard, and then looked over at the GPS display. They were blocks away from Brain Train and a few farther from Etta's apartment. But even with her faux pas, Etta wished the drive was longer.

"So, I was going to tell you this earlier, but I got a little distracted followed by a horrendous bout of humiliation." Etta looked over at Cane. Their head still faced the road, but their eyes peeked at her. "I go to this antique bookstore in Amherst often. The owner and I have become friendly. Dorian is very well-versed in old books, especially those with interesting histories. Maybe we can go together, and you can see if he knows anything about that book you mentioned earlier. A title, an author—literally anything."

The car slowed to a stop in front of Etta's apartment. Cane put it in park and turned to her smiling before wrapping their arms around her in a gentle hug. Etta reminded herself to breathe and returned the gesture.

Settling back down into the driver's seat, Cane's smile stretched wide. "Absolutely. Let's do that. That'd be great."

CHAPTER 7

———

The bus dropped Etta off in Amherst only a few blocks away from The Attic. The sun was still out, but the wind pierced through her jacket. Sinking deeper in her scarf-of-many-colors, Etta thought of how considerate Riley was for knitting it. When handing it to her, he snarked, "You're just not built for a New England winter."

And he wasn't wrong. But now Etta was acutely aware of how often she complained of being cold as this was the second person to gift her with handmade winter clothes. If she whined some more, she could probably get a hat. But in the meantime, she hunched her shoulders high, hiding her ears in the scarf, and absorbed whatever warmth the sun was willing to give.

Before leaving their apartment, Etta walked out on Sam and Riley comfortable on the couch with Cleese at their feet. She couldn't help but realize how at ease they seemed, as if they'd been together forever. As if this is how it's always been. Etta couldn't help but remark (to herself) how natural they were.

Sam wasn't going to become a hermit. Riley could never. And Cleese, who typically hated people, definitely wouldn't.

Etta on the other hand. There was still a good chance for that. At least according to Sam.

Of all the tragedies Etta assumed she'd live through, dying alone and forlorn was never one of them. Sam's words kept playing in her head like a broken record. "To have nothing and no one. It's just a sad existence."

She pictured what Dorian's home looked like. If it was anything like his office above The Attic, it was probably deranged. Even though bookshelves would line every wall, he'd still have piles hip-high scattered across tables and the floor. The overhead light would be in disrepair, so the only illumination would come from a series of desk lamps precariously perched—at least one sitting atop a book pile. And in the very corner beneath a window, Dorian would sit in a massive, velvet armchair with a book in his lap.

But besides the mass disorganization, the prospect of a cozy place to study among piles of books sounded nice. The undisturbed chance to follow the rabbit down the burrow, through the hall of doors, and past the gardens. To mystify your mind with human history told through the evolution of language. Peoples meeting; civilizations expanding and contracting as new words for old ideas spread from top to bottom. Technology developing to make it easier to share information among the masses, creating a need for society to develop their reading skills. What an enchanting corner.

Pushing the door of The Attic open, Etta walked in to Dorian stalking a patron at the far end of the store. An old man held an even older book in his hand, flipping the pages with the other; the clear wrapping crackled at every slight movement.

"You better be careful," Dorian warned, leering over the old man's shoulder and scrutinizing him with every page turn. "That book is probably worth more than your entire existence."

Etta rolled her eyes as she hung her jacket in the armoire and headed toward the French Press. At least she didn't yell at strangers in public. The old man thwopped the book shut. He turned the book over and checked the back. The lines around his mouth and on his forehead deepened as he squinted at Dorian.

"The tag says it's sixty-five." His tone was deadpan.

Dorian snatched the book in a huff. "That's not the point!" His voice grew. "This is a very important historical piece of literature. Its real value is… Well. It's invaluable!"

Etta wedged herself between the pair. A plosive *bup* popped from her lips as she pointed in prudence. Since it was the millionth time the pair ended up in this exact predicament, Dorian backed down, knowing exactly how the scene would end—with Etta berating him in front of said old man.

She gently removed the book from Dorian's hands and turned her shoulders to cut him off from the customer. "Let me assist you," she said sweetly before turning back toward Dorian. "Why don't you go upstairs or something?"

Standing his ground, Dorian glared at the old man. Etta turned fully away from him, flashing a pained smile in hopes of de-escalation. "Sir, are you interested in buying this book? Because I can go ring you up if you want."

"No, she can't," Dorian interjected, folding his arms like a cross toddler. "She doesn't work here."

"But I know how to use the register. I was bored a few weeks ago," Etta said through the corner of her mouth before softening her face. The demeanor change was almost robotic—like flipping a switch. "You can just follow me…"

The customer's face eased as he took steps toward the door. "No, that's okay, hon. I'll just leave."

The pair watched the old man make his way out. Etta sighed, trying as hard as she could. After letting the sudden adrenaline spike simmer, she looked toward Dorian who was making childish faces—still less harsh than the ones she was making in her head. He froze mid-snarl, realizing he was caught.

"What?" he asked as if it was normal for bookstore owners to yell at the elderly. Etta's eyes rolled so deep into the sockets that her head fell back before letting out an exasperated laugh. "How do you even stay in business?"

She put the book back in its place and walked to the front desk to grab her backpack and coffee. Dorian followed closely behind, muttering something about family railroad money and inheriting books from the personal collections of the Dickinson, Frost, and Dewey families.

"I put aside a stack of books you might find interesting," he commented. "They're under the counter."

As she let her cup of coffee sit on her lips before inevitably burning her tongue, Etta's eyes grew from excitement.

"You can bring some of them home to keep," Dorian continued. "I'm running out of shelf space in my personal collection and out of square footage in my apartment for another bookshelf. But leave the ones in the plastic sleeves. Those stay here!"

"So wait," Etta began with a snicker. "I can take books home—for free—from your personal collection, but that man couldn't take a book home he was going to pay for?"

Dorian snippily sneered, pushing the hair out of his eyes. "That man didn't deserve that book. He wouldn't have taken care of it," he quashed before making his way toward the stairs and into his office.

Pushing past her newly burnt tongue, Etta quickly put her cup down before spilling anything on the desk. Anything to avoid an already agitated Dorian. She pictured him stewing in his office, irate from the audacity of a paying customer. At least Etta wasn't like that. Frankly, it seemed like a waste of energy, and she was too much of a pushover to accidentally offend anyone with her inconvenient dislike.

Had Dorian always been like this? Or did he gradually become this way? Was Dorian predestined to become the cantankerous bookstore owner? Or did he grow into this? If the latter was Etta doomed to become the copywriter equivalent of the stuffy, stiff, graying librarian shushing the teens working on a group project because they were disturbing a senior reading the latest Glenn Beck book.

Etta picked up the stack of books and set them down on the counter. The first was a paperback book titled *Stories of English* by David Crystal, its cover bent and spine cracked; the second, an old hardcover collection of poems by Sir Thomas Wyatt; and the third a copy of Lucian's *Symposium*. Underneath a paperback copy of Dekker and Middleton's *The Roaring Girl* sat a sad, navy, leather-bound book with a cracked spine from over-handling.

The letters etched in the side were patchy at best, but the remaining gold had mostly rubbed or flaked off. She tried pulling the book out of the stack but managed to knock over half of the pile instead. The few closest to the top slid across the counter and the rest spilled over like a stack of oversized dominos. But as she was too entranced by the book now in her hands, Etta just left them wherever they fell.

The condition of the etchings on the front cover resembled those of the spine. A tear split the corner, revealing the binding underneath. The frays felt like thorns as Etta dragged her fingers across them, and the aged leather felt rough to the touch. She stared at the cover as if becoming entranced.

The longer she held it, the lighter it became until it began to feel like an extension of her body. Etta's eyes fixed on the engraved text. Through the fading, she could make out the title words with little trouble.

"*Vox Libri.*"

She recognized the Latin words. *Vox* meaning voice, and *Libri* as in book. She looked for an author but couldn't find one—not on the front, not on the spine, not even on the back. So she cracked the book open to its title page.

Vox Libri
Vis audire?

As she skimmed through the short passages, the floating dust shimmered like raining glitter as it caught the light. Unlike the title page, everything was in English and the illustrations seemed to dance off the page. An overwhelming wave of curiosity washed over her. Plenty of books had caught Etta's eye before, but none created such an urgency to belong to her. None fit so comfortably in her hand. She closed the book, tucked it under her arm, and then made her way up to Dorian's office.

Etta peeked through the cracked door, finding Dorian nose-deep in the old literary magazine restoration project. His office was dark except for the incredibly bright lamp, hinged out and over his head. Its glow lit up the project on his desk and his white gloves were like an opening number of a high school production of *Pippin.*

Etta knocked on the doorframe. Dorian squinted and looked up at her. He pushed his glasses to the top of his head, removed one of his gloves, and then rubbed his eyes trying to refocus his vision. She held up *Vox Libri*.

"What do you know about this book?"

Dorian squinted tighter and wheeled his squeaky metal rolling chair closer to get a better look. He held out his hand out, and Etta passed it to him. He brought it close to his face, inspecting the leather and binding. Etta's hands felt cold. She watched him open the book, delicately turning the pages before flipping back to the title page.

"*Fusce imaginatio*—Well, according to the inner cover, it's about ideas," Dorian began. "And judging by the binding, it's from the mid-1800s at least."

"Anything else?"

Book in hand, Dorian rolled over to his desk and laid it in his lap. He shuffled through the stacks of papers, files, and folders on his desk until he found what he was looking for. He opened the manilla folder under the desk lamp and read out loud.

"*Vox Libri*—bought and paid for by Dorian Melmoth of Dorian's Attic, payment made out to Gwen Fairfax. I believe I remember her telling me she acquired it from the personal library of her grandmother, but that's about all I know. I got it at an estate sale."

"Do you have her contact information? Would you be able to figure out more?"

Dorian turned and looked at Etta over his glasses, passing the book back to her. "Sure. But what specifically do you want to know about the book? Private book collectors aren't usually receptive to open-ended questions."

As she admired *Vox Libri*, it grew warm under her touch, like it had been baking in the sun for an hour. "What are its origins, for starters? Who wrote it? Stuff like that."

"No problem," Dorian responded, jotting something down on a notepad before facing back toward Etta. "Why the immense interest? You've never been this curious about a book before."

Etta shrugged. She didn't know how to explain to Dorian that it called to her. That it moved her before she'd even had the chance to read it. "I can take this one home with me. Right?" she asked.

"Not yet," he stated, taking the book out of her hands and inspecting it again. "Until we know more, I'm going to keep this one at the store."

"But it's not one of the ones covered in plastic. And you said those were the only ones I couldn't take with me."

Dorian looked back up at Etta, a smug smile spreading across his face that pulled his cheeks up to what looked like an uncomfortable inverted arch. "Yes, but this book looks really rare and incredibly difficult to find," he justified. "It could be a cult classic, and I would be incredibly foolish if I let you walk out of this store with that book for free."

Etta huffed. "Well, how much would you charge me for it?"

"Way more than you're probably willing to pay for a book," Dorian replied too quickly.

She rolled her head, the back of her crown momentarily resting at the nape of her neck, and then tried again. "How much?"

Dorian locked eyes with his only friend—or so Etta believed and hoped would take into consideration. She could see the cogs interlocking behind his stare, as if he was a dueling horologist, racing to piece together his pocket watch before her.

"Well, for a random book collector," he began, pretending to inspect the book again, "I would probably say somewhere around twelve hundred..."

"Dollars?" Etta spat. "Dorian, that's insane. You don't even know anything about the book yet."

"That's being generous," he replied. "But for you... I'd discount it to seven. And only because I know how well you'd take care of it."

"How thoughtful," she said, noting her eyes had never experienced a stretching exercise as rigorous as today.

She watched as Dorian rolled back to his desk and laid *Vox Libri* down at the edge. He put his glove back on and turned back to his old literary magazine, its weathered pages rustling against each other. Etta walked closer and placed her hand on top of the book. She stood over it for a moment, mesmerized by the light reflecting off the leather. Feeling very childlike, but unable to pull herself away, she asked, "I have to get going, but can I at least take it back downstairs and keep looking at it?"

"Of course," he said, pulling his glasses back over his eyes.

"Since you have no real intention of selling the book yet, even to me, can you at least keep it under the counter for my benefit?" Etta nearly pleaded. "I would love to study it further."

Dorian looked up at her from over his glasses and shut his eyes. "Sure."

Instinctually, Etta wanted to skip out the door, book in hand, but thought better of it, weary of Dorian's judgment.

"Thank you!" She smiled, picking the book back up and hugging it close to her body. She bounced down the stairs toward the front desk, stored it under the counter, thinking about how she'd get to tell Cane all about it on Monday, and then grabbed her stuff to head home.

CHAPTER 8

———

The weather was unseasonably warm for a February in Northampton, but Etta was grateful for the sun. With no update from Dorian, the weekend moved slower than Etta anticipated. And with not much else to do other than watch Sam and Riley come and go from the apartment while Cleese stared at her from his cat tower, Etta could only think about *Vox Libri*.

As she opened the office door and climbed the stairs, she couldn't wait to see Cane. She had to tell them about the book she found at the store. The one with the beautiful leather as blue as the midnight sky, the faded embossment like a gold bracelet tarnished by age, and the split in the binding as bottomless as the Grand Canyon. They'd understand why *Vox Libri* was all she could think about all weekend.

Vox Libri. The voice of books. The phrase floated around her mind like a tourist meandering around a lazy river as Etta walked to her desk. Both Denise and Terach were already settled in their cubicles and working, so neither one noticed her pass by.

She threw her backpack and jacket into the corner and slunk into her desk chair, spinning once before situating herself in front of the computer screen. The computer took a moment to turn on, whirring softly in a black glow before finally displaying the log-in screen. Etta pulled her words up and squinted at the next one needing editing.

"*Mnemonic*—assisting or intending to assist memory; of or relating to memory."

Etta's brain reeled like an old slide projector, word maps rapidly clicking past her vision. Its remote held by the Titan Goddess Mnemosyne, mother of the muses, overlooking the Mediterranean atop a cliffside. Realizing she'd been side-tracked for nearly ten minutes, Etta typed out "a device to assist memory; aiding one's memory" and was marginally proud she managed to knock off three words from the original definition.

Sitting back in her chair, she swiveled side to side staring at the newly edited word. Etta thought deeply about its history. Back to its home in Greece.

Vox Libri was a Latin phrase. A dead language. Meaning the book could be ancient. But if Dorian's judgment was correct, its binding dated it to the Victorians. Who notoriously idolized Ancient Rome.

Her hand darted to the mouse, promptly opening her email. There, at the top, sat a forwarded response from Dorian. Etta clicked and read.

Vox Libri came from the personal library of my great-grand-mother, Cecily. She lived for a short while in Paris where she befriended a series of aging Bohemians. Family legend says Paul Laurent was among them.

Supposedly, the pair got on so well that he welcomed Cecily into his private library, and upon his passing, bequeathed a good portion of it to her. Knowing this, when I eventually inherited Cecily's library, I had a specialist come to analyze the collection. Although she wasn't absolutely certain, the specialist suspects it's an undistributed work by Laurent's lover, Arthur Monet. She noted the style and cadence matched that in Une Inferno Promenade.

Personally, I'd never read it as an adult, but I vaguely recall my grandmother Gwendolen reading it to me as a child. I don't remember the stories, but I do remember the vibrant make-believe games we'd play afterward. In her last years, she'd become distressed when Vox Libri wasn't near her. My mother would find her clutching the book in her sleep.

Etta sat back unsatiated. Rubbing her eyes, she hoped more would magically appear once her eyes readjusted. But the confines of reality were often disappointing.

"Who knocked over your ice cream cone?" a startling voice laughed from the entrance of her cubicle. Etta fixed her glasses and spotted Cane with their mug in hand. She looked at her coworker with incredible confusion, squinting her eyes until she could barely see them. "I don't know what for, but you're sulking. That much I can see."

"It's not important," Etta quickly replied. "How was the rest of your weekend?"

"Nothing exciting," Cane began, shrugging their shoulders. "I bought my first sewing kit and learned how to repair some patches on my jacket."

"Were they falling off?"

"Yeah," Cane replied. "I try taking care of it since it's like wearing a piece of family history. What about you? What'd you do after Friday?"

Etta gestured toward her computer. "The Attic. I asked Dorian to do some research about a book for me, and he did. He answered my questions, but I guess I was hoping for more."

Cane leaned in, skimming the email. "The book we talked about the other day?"

She shook her head in response. "No, not yet. I figured we could do that when we go to The Attic together. But I found this beautiful, old book named *Vox Libri*. Dorian dated it to the mid-1800s. It was unlike anything I've ever come across."

"How so?" Cane responded before sipping their coffee.

"I honestly couldn't tell you specifics. You'll just have to see it for yourself," Etta joked.

"Well, do you have it with you?"

Etta shook her head again. "No," she griped. "Dorian wanted to charge me way too much for it on the grounds it was probably really rare. And by the sound of this email, he was right. But he's keeping it under the counter so I can look at it whenever I want."

"Why don't we go after work?" Cane suggested. Etta looked up at her smiling coworker. Feeling her insides tighten in excitement, she pressed her lips together to repress the toothiest of grins.

"I can't tonight. I promised my roommate I'd make dinner," she began, trying to mask the disappointment in her voice. "But what about tomorrow? We can go right out of work."

Cane eagerly nodded. "I'll meet you here?"

"It's a date."

CHAPTER 9

———

The door creaked as Etta escorted Cane into the store. Walking behind the counter, Etta put her jacket away in the giant wardrobe. She turned back around and noticed Cane's eyebrows raised like an unspoken question mark. Etta held her hand out to grab their jacket.

"I'm here a lot," Etta answered.

The leather of the jacket felt age-worn and soft as it rested heavily limp in her grip. She grabbed another hanger from the armoire and hung it next to her own as Cane stepped closer to the counter. Etta turned back to grab the French Press and reached for her Styrofoam cup sitting in its wonted place. She lifted the cup and started to pour, catching the exact moment in Cane's expression when they discovered Etta's name scribbled on the side.

"You're not kidding." They laughed, turning to face the rest of the store and narrowly tripping over the vacuum cleaner left carelessly on its side.

Etta graciously pretended not to see the incident but did notice the floating dust particles under the lamp on the counter and came to the conclusion Dorian had some semblance of a plan to clean The Attic but something more urgent distracted him. Truthfully, it was probably something about his restoration project. Or maybe even a question in his head adamant about being answered. Either way, Etta understood the urgency.

"Is it always this empty? And dusty?" Cane continued as Etta ducked underneath the counter, keeping to the balls of her feet and steadying herself by grasping the edge of the counter with one hand. Etta squinted through the poor light looking for *Vox Libri* among the pile of books.

"Yes," she replied, raising her voice and falling to her knees. Etta grimaced as she pulled the cuff of her cardigan over her hand and used it as a dust rag for the stack in front of her. "To both."

Clapping the residue off her sleeve, Etta wriggled her nose, now bothered by the disturbed dust. "Dorian doesn't really like people very much," she elaborated between coughs.

"The… owner, right?" Cane clarified.

Etta responded with a quick nod. "Last weekend, I caught him yelling at a customer—an old man, no less—and he practically chased him out of the store. It's not out of the ordinary. It happens often."

"But he likes you enough to put books aside for you—and a coffee?"

Etta peeked her head out from the shelves, startled to see Cane leaning over the counter. It was disconcerting to have someone else at The Attic with her. She half-expected herself to be hallucinating and speaking to an empty store the entire time. But she shrugged and continued speaking.

"Well, yeah. But I'm special." Ducking back underneath the counter, Etta sat on the floor with her legs crossed comfortably. "I'm here often, I'm quiet, and I usually stick to the back of the store with my headphones on. He's usually preoccupied with something in his office, and I don't bother him."

Etta rifled through the stack of books as she spoke, carefully picking them up one at a time and beginning another pile until she'd gone through all of them. "Sometimes he likes to show off the old literary magazine he's been restoring, or he'll show me something else he's currently excited about—usually new books he's found. You know, like antique books written in Old English, or books published on printing presses instead of laser printers."

"Okay, but..." Cane responded drawing out the last syllable as if they had more to say but hadn't fully formed the thought yet. "Why...? How'd...?"

Etta scooted back to get a better look at them. Watching the words tick through their brain, Etta feigned patience waiting for Cane to speak, their face unmistakably squirming as they tried to construct their question. Etta arched her eyebrows, goading them into asking.

"How did this become your regular spot?" Cane finally asked.

Etta paused and thought back to the first time she'd walked into The Attic.

"I guess it just kind of happened," she answered. "I'd just moved to Northampton—I don't even think I'd been there for more than a month and a half yet. I was in Amherst, visiting my friend Emily who was adjuncting for UMASS's dance program at the time. She canceled, and I didn't want to waste the trip, so I just started walking around and stumbled upon the place.

"I've always had a thing for independent bookstores and just walked in," Etta continued with a laugh. "It was dark and had that antique feeling; almost as if a significant amount of history was trapped here. It had this days-of-yore charm, like the rest of Massachusetts generally does. I'm really drawn to that sort of thing. But this place just felt important, and I felt comfortable. So I kept coming back."

"But how'd you become friendly with the owner?" Cane pushed, sounding bemused.

"Actually," Etta began. "I was browsing through the stacks and was thumbing through a book when he snuck up and accosted me. I can't exactly remember, but I'm positive he questioned me on what I knew about the book I was holding and was taken aback when I was actually able to answer. We started talking from there—mostly about bizarre language stuff. And when I kept coming back, he didn't chase me out. He'd smile and wave or show me the latest book he'd bought, and it sort of escalated from there."

Etta stared blankly for a moment underneath the counter. Scanning the shelf behind her, she spotted the navy book wedged among others. "Here it is!" she exclaimed, popping back up to put the book on the counter. Cane reached over and pulled it closer to them, tracing the faded etching with their fingertips. Etta turned on a second lamp as Cane opened the book and slowly thumbed through the pages.

"*I sit on the cliffside, overlooking the sound,*" Cane read aloud. "*The unearthed mirror reflects Apollo chasing away Artemis, golden gilly glittering across the horizon. The echo of the waves and myself roar below. O freedom of Faroe that which France forsakes!*"

Shutting her eyes, Etta let the words wash over her. She pictured the Danish islands and could feel the sea breeze on her face with the waves cracking against the cliffs.

Cane went quiet for a moment. Opening her eyes, Etta watched as they stared blankly over the counter, their face solemn. Cane saw something in front of them Etta couldn't see, and she wondered what it was. Cane's eyes shut for a moment and opened back up to meet Etta's and then they smiled. "It's wonderful," they uttered.

"Etta?"

They looked up from *Vox Libri* and saw Dorian coming down from his office with a confused look on his face. Etta smiled at him and walked around the counter, standing next to Cane.

"Hey," she greeted. Cane turned away from the book, watching as Dorian continued grumpily down the staircase and walked over toward them. "This is Cane. We work together at Brain Train. I wanted to show them that book I found last week, plus they wanted to ask you about a different book."

Dorian nodded and watched Cane shift their weight.

"Actually," Cane continued warily, "I was thinking of buying *Vox Libri.*"

Etta's head jerked toward Cane. She was familiar with impulse purchasing, but nothing more expensive than her new freestanding dishwasher. She looked back at Dorian whose features squeezed together at the center of his face.

"It's not in your price range," Dorian dismissed, moving to take the book from the counter.

Etta closed the book and defensively dragged it closer to her body.

"Well, what's your asking price?" Cane said.

Dorian looked over at Cane skeptically. "Fifteen hundred dollars."

"Fifteen hundred?" Etta blurted out. "You were going to sell it to me for less than half that!"

Dorian shrugged and squared his shoulders toward Cane, standing about a foot shorter than them in what should have been an intimidating pose. The two glared at each other, stuck in a possible staring contest. Etta couldn't really tell, but she rolled her eyes and made a face in response. "What a wonderful demonstration of the fragility of an ego," she mumbled under her breath. "I'm swooning with adoration." Etta grabbed her cup of coffee and made her way to her usual table with *Vox Libri* under arm, giving Dorian and Cane enough space to assert themselves over one another. Walking through the stacks, she listened to their voices growing fainter as they argued over the price of the book. Soon enough, they were too far away to figure out who had the upper hand.

Etta took in a sizable amount of coffee, finishing off the cup, and then tossed it into the wastebasket at the foot of the table. She thought it better to finish her drink than to risk spilling any on the book. Dorian would have her head on a stake and plant it at the front of his store with a sign hanging from her neck reading: *To the careless; ye be warned*—semicolon unquestionably necessary.

The chair creaked under Etta's weight from cheap wood and old screws as she pulled herself in. She flipped through the book and landed on the remaining passage Cane hadn't read yet.

A puffinry perches, a carte blanche colony, an improbability of impunity. With a push, the wheel wings flap, flutter, fly far beyond my sight. Onward to the expanse, soon to plunge below, forming the buoying raft I wish to ride away from shore.

But no, nothing. They sail, I slump.

It is quite clear I am to remain leery, longing, and landlocked.

Curse science! For lack of evolutionary progress that I can't join
those with whom I belong. My head is full of places inaccessible.
And I remain cliffside.

Etta's head hung back as she closed her eyes. She steadied
herself with a deep breath and listened for any sign of other
people in The Attic. The quiet ballooned in her ears until she
began to hear the whispering of waves as if someone held
a seashell up to her ear. A soft breeze brushed against her
cheeks. The stale air of The Attic melted away and the chill
of a cool, wet atmosphere settled around her body.

A bright light pierced through her eyelids like the sun
shining through the parting clouds. Etta struggled to open
her eyes, straining against the blinding light. But once they
adjusted, she stood at the edge of a steep cliff. In front of her,
she saw nothing but crystalline gray water. Behind her, only
forest green and brown hills with cliffs jutting straight into
the sky. Instinctually, her arms stretched out as far as they
could on either end. Whether she would sink or soar, Etta
didn't care. Either way, she would fly.

The wind swelled beneath her and with one firm push,
Etta took off over the side and soared through the air. The
open sky was inviting, releasing a liberated zeal that flooded
through her senses. Drifting above the sound, she spotted
a grass-roofed village between the valley of two mountains
and watched a farmer herd his sheep toward an open field.

Flying did not have a weightless sensation. Instead, it felt
more like swimming, less like floating. It took more effort,
and floating was effortless. Etta became acutely aware of her
body—of her ability to sink and plummet to the ground if she
paused for a moment. Little by little, the wind resistance less-
ened, and Etta felt herself descending. In a frenzy, her instincts

kicked in. She pierced her hands through the air like a blade and then pushed the wind behind her, propelling herself up and forward. With each kick and every stroke, Etta flew higher and higher until she could feel the air become thin again.

The wind cut past Etta's face like swimming underwater. Giant gusts felt like waves crashing over her body, disorienting her sense of direction. So she rolled with the breeze like she did with the waves as a child. Remembering how she loved getting lost in the waves, Etta invited the current to break over her and drag her away, unsure of where she would inevitably end up. When she finally tumbled to the shore, she opened her eyes, picked the rocks out of her hair, and then sharply turned back around. As she ran alongside the breeze, the edge of the cliff drew closer and closer. Then with another thrust, Etta launched herself straight into the open sky.

The draft shifted, and Etta again let it take her wherever. It didn't matter. This was the freest she'd felt since childhood. The nostalgia felt like ice frozen in a pothole, filling the void with a solid, frozen mass pressing outward, eroding the hole's walls and becoming larger and larger until Etta began freefalling.

Terrified, adrenaline snapped open Etta's eyes. *Vox Libri* lay open and disappointment weighed her heavily in the chair. The immediate change in pressure and gravity spun her head in circles. She grabbed onto the desk to steady herself and took a much-needed breath, sinking lower into the chair and relieving herself of the disillusionment submerged deep in her chest.

She sat bewildered. Sanity and logic reminded her that she was sitting in The Attic. But mere moments before, reality told her she was flying above the Faroe Islands. Placing her hand over her pounding heart, she listened for either Cane or Dorian's distant voices but couldn't hear anything. Her ears strained to find any hint as to what happened between the two, even something as little as Dorian's footsteps on the stairs leading to his office. But she heard nothing. The silence made her incredibly anxious. With *Vox Libri* in hand, Etta scrambled to the front of the store finding Cane leaning on the counter by their elbows but no Dorian.

"There you are," Cane said, greeting Etta with a smile. "I was wondering where—"

"Please tell me he sold you the book," she interrupted, suddenly desperate to have it in her possession—or at least in her vicarious possession. "Dorian!" Etta called, springing toward the bottom of the stairs. "If you're not going to sell it to them, sell it to me!"

"Etta..." Cane said, following closely behind.

"I'll even pay the full asking price!" she continued.

"You don't have to do th—"

"Stop yelling!" Dorian's shouted. "Cane already bought the damn book. Jesus! You have never been this irritating before..."

The door to Dorian's office slammed shut. Turning toward Cane, Etta's eyes widened as she cradled *Vox Libri* tightly, that nostalgic ice forming the first beads of sweat.

"Really?" she nearly whispered, Cane nodding along.

Etta walked up to Cane, resting the side of her head on their shoulder in an armless hug while still holding onto the book. Wrapping their arms around Etta, Cane completed the embrace. The lingering weightlessness inside her was grounding as Etta settled herself, leaning more heavily into Cane. She could feel her heartbeat mending to its natural rhythm. Slowly realizing the two had never had this much physical contact before, Etta's body began to tense up.

"Sorry," she excused, wriggling herself free. Cane's hand remained on her shoulder.

"It's okay." Cane smiled.

Avoiding Cane's eyes, Etta stared at *Vox Libri* for a long moment. "I just can't believe he actually sold it to you," she continued softly. Etta cleared her throat and spoke at a normal volume, her voice lilting. "I've been coming here almost once a week for over a year now, and I don't think I've ever seen Dorian sell anything to anyone."

"Well," Cane said, their smile widening, "it may be my first time here, but I'm tenacious and wasn't leaving without that book."

"Well then," Etta replied, "color me impressed."

"Looks like you're not the only special one around here." Cane teasingly removed the book from Etta's hands and walked to the counter. They leaned over the ledge, their head straining as if looking for something. Etta watched Cane from the armoire, their brow furrowed from being unsuccessful. They planted themself off the counter and turned toward Etta feigning an uncomfortable grin. "Can I get a bag or something?"

Etta reached into the armoire for the pile of plastic bags on the top shelf. Pulling one apart from the rest, she handed it to Cane.

"Hey, I'm starving," Cane said, interrupting the absolute silence in the shop. "What's good around here?"

CHAPTER 10

———

Walking out to the streets of Amherst was like stepping off a space shuttle and into the sky. Or so Etta imagined. Whatever comfort and warmth had settled under her layers from the few hours spent at The Attic now disappeared as if ripped from her body. She thought back to the winters growing up when the sun would set and vacuum the little heat along with it. However, this was an entirely new level of wintry. It was damn near glacial. But Etta currently didn't mind. She was preoccupied.

With *Vox Libri* under her arm, her senses heightened. Moments ago, she was soaring through the sky, her nerve endings electrified. The streetlights refracted off the frost-coated parking meters, sparkling like fallen glitter on a stage. Each tree relaxed with a sigh as she strolled past, and the wind tingled against her cheek, sharper now than before.

Etta looked over her shoulder, fixating on the leather sleeve with the round, patriot patch as it edged closer and closer. At the end of the sleeve was an emphatic hand, dancing along to the tale of a young kid and their two sisters. Each was named after an important moment from their mother's life—Minnie for the stuffed doll gifted by their father; Sue from learning conversational English by watching *Three's Company;* and, in hopes of a boy, Cane after the sugarcane stalks she'd suckle as a child on her grandparent's farm.

Etta followed the length of the sleeved arm until she saw Cane's equally expressive face. The top of their long neck was partially exposed from the tucked-in scarf, and their short, dark hair lay straight, flattened by a knitted beanie. Etta waited for an opening, desperate to detail what she just experienced. But the cast of the streetlight would catch Cane's face, revealing their well-worn laugh lines, and Etta studied more intently, focusing instead on the sweet, warmed syrup spilling from Cane's eyes.

"*Bleh,* sorry," Cane interrupted themself, comically contorting their face. For the second time that day, Etta experienced the weight of gravity hurling her back down to the earth. "No more mood killers. We have *Vox Libri.* I own it. We can read it whenever we want. It's a happy day! Not a retrospection of past loves."

Etta nodded slowly, turning her head. Surprised by the strength of her autopilot, she rewound the footage from the last ten minutes. As she projected it onto the screen in her mind, silent clips of aesthetically pleasing images played back. The remorse from distraction clenched its hand around her stomach, tightening its grasp by the second.

"But thanks for letting me babble," Cane continued. "You're a good listener."

She sheepishly smiled in response, desperately trying to hide her embarrassment. Etta was now rid of any urgency to share. She'd have time to do so later. For now, they had *Vox Libri* and that's what mattered.

The pair advanced up the block, the sleeves of their jackets brushing against one another. Jumping in front of Etta, Cane pulled the red door open. The whitewashed brick made the space appear larger than it was. The longer they stood inside, the more the lingering smell of the earthy roasts grounded Etta in her surroundings. Stopping in front of the counter, they looked up at the menu and studied the pastry case.

"I thought you said they had food here," Cane whispered, turning their head away from the waiting barista.

"They do!" Etta pointed to the stacked croissants, scones, and uncooked bougie grilled cheese.

"We also sell a meat and cheese plate," the barista interrupted.

Cane slowly raised their eyebrows and tightened their lips before turning back toward Etta. "I mean, it's almost 7 p.m. I'm gonna need some real food. Also, are you sure coffee is a good idea right now?"

Etta scoffed. "Coffee is always a good idea."

Cane closed their eyes and flashed a bemused smile. "Then let's make a deal," they began. "We order to-go, hop in my car, and then grab real food and head back to my condo. We can eat and read and then I can drive you home."

Etta eagerly cut in front of Cane, deciding this was a sufficient enough response. She situated herself accordingly, her shoulders bending over the granola bars and hips nearly touching the counter, prattling off her order before pointing toward her new friend.

"Ew, tea?" Etta gagged, sticking out her tongue like a dramatic child causing a scene over some cough medicine.

"Not everyone can metabolize caffeine the way you do. Okay?"

Snickering to herself, Etta swiped her card, threw a dollar into the tip jar, and walked with Cane to the pick-up counter. A percussion-heavy song softly played throughout the shop causing Etta's pulse to mimic the drumbeat—hard, rhythmic, and plosive.

"This place is cute," Cane mentioned, looking around the shop.

"It's kind of my second favorite place in Massachusetts."

"The first being?"

"The Attic—when Dorian's not being an ass, that is." Etta laughed, waiting for Cane to snicker along with her, but instead found their face blank. "How'd you convince him to sell to you?"

Cane looked back at Etta, their face warming until they looked bemused. Their voice became gruff. "I don't back down from bullies."

"A bully?" Etta nervously laughed. "I don't know if I'd go that far…"

"No? For real? Then what would you call that?" They snorted. "You even said yourself you don't think you've seen him sell to anyone before."

Etta felt her insides shrink. Up until now, she'd never considered Dorian as anything other than greatly protective and wildly passionate. And now here was a second person criticizing him. But unlike Sam, Cane had met Dorian. They experienced it firsthand.

"Not to pull the-customer-is-always-right card," Cane continued, seemingly unaware of Etta's uneasiness, "but that is one, not normal for a shop owner; two, not okay if he's trying to run a successful shop; but three, indicative of a sad, lonely hermit."

Etta fell silent. There it was again. *Hermit.* She turned her attention to the changing drumbeat over the speakers, which felt like it'd been injected straight into her ears. She felt her eyes glaze over Cane's shoulder to stare at the white-painted bricks of the wall.

"Etta?" She shook off the dissociation and looked toward her friend. Cane wore a concerned expression before asking, "You okay?"

"Mm-hmpf. Yep. All good." The words scattered out of her mouth like ants rushing back to their colony. "You're just not the first person to call Dorian a hermit. Sam also has. 'Reclusive' was his word, actually. Not lonely. But they're not far off from each other." A panicked laugh escaped her chest, releasing some of the tightness before hastily taking in another breath, her ribcage compressing her lungs again. "He's even gone so far as to accuse me of being a hermit too! Isn't that… just peak situational comedy?"

Etta's head began to spin. She could feel her pounding pulse at the crook of her neck. It had almost been a full year since Etta felt this way. Her vision began to darken, and in the distance, she could almost make out the confines of her childhood bedroom. At the foot of the bed sat Etta from just over a year ago, in the exact moment Northampton went from thought to decision.

"But, like you said, this is a happy time!" she continued, her voice hitting octaves she didn't know were possible. "We need to celebrate! Coffee, food, and reading—it's gonna be great!"

"Right…" Cane responded, awkwardly chuckling. "Maybe let's hold off on drinking the coffee until we get some food in us?"

Etta looked toward the end of the counter and pointed to the sweating water dispenser. "Maybe I should…"

"Probably a good idea." Cane nodded.

Etta sipped slowly from her cup, letting the chilled water sit in her cheeks. The bagged *Vox Libri* pressed deeper into her chest. The pressure allowed her to focus long enough to take a steadying breath. Returning to Cane, she gaped at their sympathetic smile and then settled by their side.

Cane reached for *Vox Libri* and slipped it from the bag hooked on the crook of Etta's elbow. Holding it, they inspected the book and then settled the spine in their hand about to crack it open.

"Don't—" Etta sharply warned. Cane's eyes opened wide before reflecting their confusion. "Here's not the place," Etta lowered her voice, her eyes darting around their immediate surroundings. The barista neared with their coffee and tea in hand and rested them on the counter in front of the pair. Etta politely smiled and grabbed their drinks. She looked up at Cane, their eyes growing wide. An uneasiness of not being believed flooded her already tightened stomach, forcing itself through like a slow-moving pool of sludge. "I'm pretty sure this is *that* book."

Cane's mouth parted, and they squinted their eyes. Their head extended, prompting Etta to continue. But instead of explaining herself, Etta motioned toward the door with a tilt of her head as she slowly backed up toward it, keeping her eyes on Cane to make sure they didn't open the book in public.

Bounding out the door, Etta pulled Cane by their elbow, forcing them out quicker. She linked arms with Cane and ducked her head beneath their shoulder, still wary of eavesdroppers. Cane lowered their head as well.

"It's true," Etta repeated. "It's real."

CHAPTER 11

Etta felt her body jerk forward like a crash-test dummy hitting an invisible wall. She looked back to see an unmoving Cane, and her wrist locked around Cane's elbow. Etta stared at *Vox Libri* under Cane's opposite arm.

"What do you mean the urban legend is true?"

Etta's attention was split. The refraction from the streetlights on the gold-leaf cover wavered from Cane's slight swaying, like the prey of a king cobra, entrancing Etta. But the sense of danger still remained. Her eyes darted across the surrounding area; no one was close enough to hear. But even if they were, at worst she'd run the risk of being thought of as a random screwball. And the likelihood of anyone recognizing her as such was slim. Etta prepped herself with a deep breath.

"When I snuck away at The Attic, I finished the passage you read aloud. It went on about puffins. They jumped off a cliff and started flying. And the narrator wished they could fly." Her words got faster the longer she spoke. "Then, my eyes… I closed them. And then there was wind on my cheeks and all over, and I felt like I was on a rollercoaster with the loops and the corkscrews. And I open my eyes—or I thought I opened my eyes—and I'm flying. I was flying!

"No." Etta stopped, pointing her finger at Cane. "Don't look at me like that. I know what I saw. I know what I felt."

"Etta," Cane began, lowering their voice and gently laying their hand on Etta's shoulder. "You may be overcaffeinated. How about we get some food and more water in you?"

Ushering her into their car, Cane placed the book on the backseat and then said they were going to run up the block to grab their dinner. They'd be back. Etta felt like an invalid. Had isolation already begun to take its toll? Was she going to forego misanthropy altogether and dive straight into delusion? She should probably avoid rooms with yellow wallpaper.

Cane turned a corner and pulled through the gatehouse. The car crawled up the curvy streets lined with waist-high hedges. The buildings in the complex resembled the iconic Number Four Privet Drive home but were crammed to accommodate as many as possible in the modest location.

"I was lucky in finding this place," Cane said, pointing out their door and then pulling away from it.

"There was a spot right out…"

"Visitor spot," they explained. The ride had been so quiet, Etta dismissed the tone-filled interruption. She was grateful for the sound. "Everyone gets two designated spots—one out front for guests and then one 'round back. I could park out front, but I grew up in a home where front doors were mostly just for guests. Back and side doors were for family."

Cane turned another corner. Behind the houses were tall wooden fences and a small lot. Cane pulled into their parking spot, and the two exited the car. Etta felt heavy, as if the winter air became thick and weighted. And even with a coffee still in hand, she felt tired. Her breath became shallow, each one softly tugging at her eyelids.

She watched Cane reach back into the car to grab *Vox Libri*. Cane then jogged in front of her to open the gate to the little backyard. A tiny garden was set up along the fence, ready for warmer weather. A garden table and outwardly turned chairs sat in the corner by the back door. An ashtray sat too close to the edge.

"When it's nice outside, I like to sit outside and eat or read or hang and stargaze. And I grow tomatoes and peppers when it's warm. Sometimes I've got a planter pyramid of different herbs growing over there." Etta nodded as well as she could.

"I really like basil. Plus, I heard basil is actually really great for the bee population, so two birds," Cane noted walking through their yard toward the door. They fumbled with the keys before managing to get it opened and then welcomed Etta inside.

Cane gestured to a well-loved velvet couch, laid *Vox Libri* on the scarf-covered coffee table, and then disappeared through the kitchen archway. Etta took a seat and watched the cushions change from a green apple to a darker olive color after running her hand across them. She looked around the room, its walls covered from top to bottom with photographs, shelves of books and trinkets, and potted plants with hanging vines. Etta found quiet in the noise of the satisfying maximalism. Misfit tchotchkes filled every bare surface with no rhyme, reason, or motif like the inside of an antique shop. Everything was equally in and out of place. Cane made a home for things that either could not find one before or had lost theirs.

Etta's heart thumped along with the plate Cane placed in front of her. Cane chuckled and held out a fork. She took it between her fingers then chased a cherry tomato around her plate.

"I know what I saw," Etta muttered like a question, the doubt of what she'd experienced settling deeper than before. Her fork hand swung down like an ax, catching the tomato by its skin and projectile launching it off the plate. It rolled under the rosy wingback.

"I mean, have you been getting enough sleep?" Cane began, their voice hesitant. "I know when I'm overtired, I can get pretty loopy."

"I know what I saw," Etta repeated, louder this time. The salty air lingered heavily, sitting near the back of her throat. "I was flying. Above cliffs and water and a village. It was real."

With just a look, Etta tried to convey her earnestness, but her desperation was palpable. Cane pushed the plates away and pulled *Vox Libri* closer. They opened to a random passage and began to read out loud.

"Life's breath is still within Bohemia! Its spirit persists, protesting the predeterminism of the Philistines. Their calls for perfection fall upon deaf ears, its failure fortune's fate. For man does not thrive within such confines, nor does he have such access.

"Progress is the ambition. Artists the new nobility. The world pushes forward on to a beautiful, unfettered future of love and honor.

"Hear them celebrate. See them dance. Feel the unbreakable spirit continue on for centuries to come."

A cool white cone spotlighted the coffee table as the pages of *Vox Libri* fanned out with a *thworp*. Etta and Cane sat stunned. A rhythmic snare hissed a *tss-t-t-tss* as a hand slowly stretched itself from behind the unfurled pages. In the background, a horn began to croon and the wrist began to roll. Its fingers curled slowly into the palm one by one. A second hand appeared beneath the book to hold it at its spine.

"*Meine Damen und Herren*," an animated voice called as the lights in Cane's apartment began to dim. "*Die Varieté-Burleske...*"

An orchestra filled with percussion and brass boiled to a stewed volume as the bottom hand flipped the open book, page-side down, and the second one disappeared underneath the spectacle. The remaining hand shimmied the spine as a sprinkling of glitter rained from the pages. Feathers sprouted from the binding of *Vox Libri* until it no longer appeared like a book. The hand fluttered the now-feathered fan and enticingly pulled it upward to slowly reveal sparkling shoes, fishnetted legs, a rhinestoned bustier, and the face of a victory-rolled ginger with ruby lips and a beauty mark.

Enamored with the star before them, Etta could not look away. She lifted her hand and felt around as if blind, looking for any piece of Cane and needing to have proof that Cane was seeing this too. She cupped above their knee and squeezed. Without breaking her gaze from the fan dancer, she felt Cane's hand rest upon her own, returning the clutch.

Above them, the dancer stood on the coffee table under the glowing spotlight. The rumble of the drums grew louder and the horns continued wailing. With each inflection of the band, the star tantalized her audience with a new swivel of her hips, a twist of her wrist, or a choreographed conceal of her fan.

With each passing second, the lights illuminated the room in a red glow and the vintage-fringed lamp shades began to shake. Just as with the fan dancer before them, burlesque dancers snaked their way through the shades until they reseted around their waists like fringed skirts. Each performer twisted, stretched, posed, and twirled while the sequins and jewels sewn into their costumes shimmered under the reddening lights.

Then the music cut, and the room went dark.

"Hiya callit... Der 'trommelwirbel,' auf Englisch?" muttered the thickly German accented voice. Etta listened closely for a reply before the disembodied voice shouted, "Drumroll, please!" as a deep, coppery drumroll resonated through the air.

A spotlight snapped to the corner of the room, revealing a modestly dressed woman performatively sulking at a vanity, and the drums stopped. She stared at her reflection, head in hand, and melodramatically sighed. In the background, a lone trombone moaned out a bluesy tune. The shattering of glass and arguing was discernible from off stage. The woman looked toward the commotion, her face growing more vividly concerned. With a sudden movement, she whipped out a trunk lined with buckles and tossed articles of clothing inside. Defiantly snapping it shut, she looked toward the uproar before taking off in the opposite direction, bringing the spotlight with her.

A mirror along the wall melted into a marquee in front of Etta and Cane reading *Die Varieté-Burleske.* Underneath the sign stood a frail man in an oversized suit, bowler hat, and cane. The woman from the previous scene ran straight up to him. She silently begged and pleaded with him as other horns chimed in with the trombone. The suited man tucked the cane under his arm, removed his hat, and bowed low enough to draw focus to the worn-out spats over his shoes. The woman giddily jumped and clapped, and then she ran through the double doors under the marquee.

Standing upright, the man turned toward Etta and Cane and smirked. He cupped his hand by his mouth and whispered, "*Das Finale*," before disappearing behind the doors himself.

The lights momentarily grew dim before flashing brilliantly along with the accompaniment. The music grew brighter and livelier as the burlesque dancers reappeared. They parted in the middle to reveal the simple woman holding the feathered fan behind her back. She outstretched her arms until the fan was above her head and then figure-eighted it down until she was totally concealed. Then just as before, the fan shimmied upward, slowly revealing the same fan dancer from the start of the show.

With a final flick of their fringe-clad hips, the burlesque dancers threw their hands in the air as if to swan dive away. But instead, they wound their hips from side to side until all that remained were the original, fringed Victorian lampshades.

The star laid her fan back on the table and climbed back inside. She wriggled her nose, coyly smirked, and gave the pair a wink before disappearing entirely. The fan snapped closed, a gust of glitter blowing in its wake. When it settled, the cool stage lighting faded back to the apartment's natural warm tones. *Vox Libri* lay face-down on the table.

They sat together in silence, both gawking at the book, enamored at the spectacle they'd just witnessed. Etta heard Cane take a settling breath and turned to look at them. Their eyes were wide, nearly popping out of their head. Their pupils swallowed their irises revealing only a small cinnamon ring. They inched sideways until they stared at Etta.

"Told ya so."

CHAPTER 12

——

Etta's travel mug of coffee lay close to her chest in a near-death grip of her gloved fingers. Her steps echoed up the staircase as they did every morning, each one more exhausting than the next. She reached the top of the stairs, opened the door to her floor, and slunk into the office. As she walked past their cubicles, she forced a smile to Denise and Terach, yanking the corners of her mouth as high as they would go to feign polite interaction but feeling the weighted resistance of exhaustion. She then dumped everything onto her spare chair before collapsing into her own, laying her head down on the desk.

"Tired?" she heard Cane say before rolling her head to see theirs poking above the cubicle wall.

Etta nodded in response before laying her forehead back down.

"I told you not to drink that last cup of coffee." Cane laughed, bags deep set around their eyes as well.

"How'd that tea work out for you?" Etta snarked.

"Wow," Cane replied wryly. "I never realized how very not pleasant you are in the morning."

Etta turned her head again and glared at Cane under drowsy, hooded eyes. "Back off," she muttered.

Cane snickered and headed toward the breakroom.

After leaving Cane's, Etta couldn't settle. Her brain was too wired. As one spark of excitement fizzled, another detail flashed in her mind—another rhinestone, a different cloud—repeatedly until the sun rose. As such, Etta felt twice as heavy as usual, especially compared to her ethereal near-weightlessness from the day before. But she still couldn't wait to unlock what else *Vox Libri* had to offer.

Etta rested her head on her desk for another minute before listening to the office wake up, beginning to make moves for the day. She lifted her hefty head and rubbed her neck, pulling up her work files and email. At the top of her inbox sat a message from Cane with the subject title *AGNES*.

"Code-switching: changing seamlessly between two languages within a single conversation," the top of the email began. *Remember the emcee last night? Specifically right before the second act and the drumroll. He shouted something that wasn't German or English...*

Etta thought back to the spectacle of last night. She remembered the colors, the sequins, the lights, the music, and the dancers, but she barely remembered the emcee. She turned her attention back to the email.

Have you ever heard Agnes ask, 'What do you call it?'

Thinking again, she couldn't recall any time Agnes fumbled for a word and asked, "What do you call it?" English was Agnes's second language, but she'd lived in the States for decades and had a firm grasp of it. She was never really at a loss for words; in fact, the complete opposite. But before she could write off Cane's email and get back to her work, she received a reply.

Come to the breakroom right before lunch and listen for 'hiya callit.'

Etta exited out of her email, opened up her Scrabble games, and played *irate* for five points against Denise before switching her attention to work.

Oftentimes while working, she'd come across a word she'd never heard before. And being the admirer of language that she was, it was difficult to tap into her self-discipline skills to stay on task.

Miko, for example. She found it near impossible to ignore its history and focus strictly on its definition. "A Japanese priestess or female shaman, frequently a virgin, who acts as oracle for and handmaiden to the deity of a particular shrine and performs sacred ritual dances." Etta was sure the word would be easily glossed over or dismissed by Brain Train's users. The definition could give the reader an understanding of the noun, but its etymology gave the word such deeper meaning. Without it, why would they care? Why would they remember it?

Mi- most likely came from the Japanese suffix of *kami* meaning "divine spirit," but *-ko* probably came from the Japanese word *ko* meaning "child." So even though the definition mentioned the sexual status of a miko, it lacked the implication that this person was a child and given such an unforgettable, heavy responsibility. So from there, Etta fell down the Wikipedia rabbit hole.

"Psst!"

Etta jumped in her seat, her heart skipping a beat. She grabbed her chest and turned to see Cane standing at her cubicle opening. Her eyes widened as if to say, "Fuck you," and Cane just laughed again.

"Damn, you're jumpy," they said over her laugh while stepping inside. "Did you get my emails?"

"Yeah," Etta replied, her pulse finally steadying. She dropped her volume to a half-whisper. "But I have no idea what you're talking about. I don't think I've ever witnessed Agnes at a loss for words."

"Just wait." Cane gestured toward the breakroom. Begrudgingly standing up, Etta followed closely behind them.

Cane walked to the coffee machine, beginning to brew a pot as Etta took a seat at the table. Cane reached into the cupboard to grab two mugs, gesturing one toward Etta. She replied with a mocking vomit face, and Cane turned to put the second mug back.

"It's really not that bad. Promise."

Etta pretended to vomit again, and the two laughed.

"Odette!" Agnes nearly cheered. "You're here again! What a delight!"

"I needed to give my eyes a break from the computer." She nodded, hyper-focusing on Agnes's accent.

Agnes walked over to the refrigerator to grab her yogurt and took a seat next to Etta. Peeling off the lid, Agnes started on a story about her grandson.

"So then, Marcus ran over to the clown and made it so he would kneel down to his height," Agnes explained—her *W*s coming out like *V*s, her *N*s ending sharply, and her *TH*s sounding like *D*s. "And with one swift pull, Marcus ripped his wig off!"

Cane stood at the coffee machine laughing appropriately along whereas Etta was not. She was too focused on studying Agnes's enunciation that her laugh response was delayed. Thankfully Agnes didn't notice and continued.

"It was one of my family's better birthday parties," Agnes finished with a smile on her face, spooning yogurt toward her mouth. However, instead, she hit the crease of her lips and spilled the glob on her khaki slacks. "Ach! *Scheisse!*"

Both Cane and Etta's eyes widened and looked at each other in shock. Neither spoke German, but it wasn't a surprise to either that the other knew the foreign slur.

Agnes slapped her hand over her mouth, her cheeks reddening under the heavy rouge. "Excuse my words, please," she stammered.

Cane reached behind themselves to rip off a piece of paper towel. They walked over to the sink and dampened it before handing it over.

"Seriously, don't worry about it," Cane reassured her.

Agnes shook her head and muttered some inaudible things, presumably in German, as she cleaned off the yogurt.

"Such a mess," she muttered. "Such a klutz."

"Not really," Etta added, her voice softening. "If you could see all the spastic things I do in my cubicle throughout the day... Seriously, thank god we're partitioned off. I'm an actual embarrassment sometimes."

Agnes paused and smiled at Etta. "Dear," she laughed, "it's no secret you're the office klutz. I believe I hear you smack your knee on the desk leg at least twice a day."

Etta went to protest but knew she couldn't. Cane covered their mouth, trying to hold back how hard they wanted to laugh.

"I might be the new office spaz." Agnes laughed as she threw the paper towel out.

"Not true," Cane offered. "I hear Odette curse under her breath at least once a week because she's spilled or dropped something. If we were to do Office Superlatives, Odette would unanimously win that title." They chuckled, playfully punching Etta in the shoulder. "No questions asked."

Agnes wrapped her arm around Etta like a relative offering comfort. "We kid because we care," she said, her accent growing warm and soft as the arm-wrap turned into a hug. Agnes looked over her shoulder toward the clock on the wall. "Ach. I should be going back to work. The definitions won't edit themselves."

Agnes scurried out of the room, her steps growing fainter as she neared her cubicle. Cane poured the coffee into their cup and took a seat next to Etta. They stared knowingly as they took a sip, their face smug. Etta glared back.

"What?" Cane asked, lowering their mug.

"She didn't say it."

"Say what?"

Etta's eyes grew larger and her mouth dropped a little. "Are you serious?" Etta responded, involuntarily laughing. Cane made a sardonic face and shook their head as they took another sip. "For real? The whole reason we came in here to begin with?"

"Still don't know what you're talking about," they teased.

"*Hiya callit?*" Etta continued, raising her voice.

Cane shrugged and put their mug down on the table. "Well, I don't know what you were really expecting," they joked. "I can't control what she says and when she says it."

"You're an ass." Etta tilted her head to the side, looking at Cane. "Well, then what the hell does *hiya callit* mean?"

"You're the etymologist," they replied, lifting their coffee to take another sip. "Take a second to think about it."

Etta sat glaring for a moment before actually putting some thought behind it. She slowed the fake words down in her head. Each syllable appeared in her mind like the title card of a silent film. *Hi-ya call-it.* She pictured the emcee from last night's performance, opening his hands as if presenting the phrase. *Hi-ya.* The picture cut to him cartoonishly waving to the audience. *Call-it.* Hand next to his mouth, the emcee pantomimed a holler to each side of the screen. *Hi*-you call it… *Hi*… How? How you call it?

"Does she mean to say, 'how do you call it'? Like 'how do you say…?'" Etta asked, the emcee bowing deeply before the screen in her mind faded to black.

Cane nodded. "Isn't it great?" they replied, the excitement rising in their voice. "Now you just have to hear her say it. It's magical."

Etta stood up and pushed her chair in. "I'm going back to my desk," she stated, walking out of the room.

"You're grumpy when you don't drink three cups of coffee," Cane jokingly called after her.

Settling back into her office chair, Etta paid extra attention to the placement of the desk leg so as to not smack her knee into it like she apparently did so frequently. She turned on her sleeping computer, opened her Scrabble game, and noticed she lost the game when Denise played *urgent* for thirty-three points after placing the *G* on a triple word score. Etta sighed as the notification for a rematch popped up. She clicked yes, playing *timely* for eight points.

"*Psst,*" Etta heard coming from behind her. She turned around to see Cane's head popping out of the entrance of her cubicle again. "*Vox Libri* and dinner later?" they asked.

"You're ridiculous," Etta replied, turning back to her computer.

"That wasn't a no, though! I was thinking Thai?"

Etta opened up her work tabs. "Sounds good."

"Awesome," Cane answered. "And think of it this way, not only do you get Thai food *and* get to see what else the book has to share, but you won't have to walk home in the freezing cold."

Etta looked over her shoulder at Cane's smug, smiling face. "You raise a good point," she said, her own face softening. Cane laughed before heading back to their own cubicle.

The end of the day slowly came as if individual grains of sand slipped toward the bottom half of an hourglass in slow motion. Denise beat Etta three more times before Etta reclaimed her winning streak, and she still managed to get through a couple hundred definitions in the process. Anything to distract herself from the quaking anticipation of getting to see what else *Vox Libri* had in store.

She glimpsed her hand. The vibrating wasn't just in her head. Etta jerked her trembling hands from the keyboard, rattling them at her side like shaking off excess water. A jolt flitted up her spine, causing her head to tick. She clenched her jaw and closed her eyes to wait for the sensations to pass.

"Productive day?"

Etta jerked in her chair. She turned to see Cane's disembodied head hovering over the entrance of her cubicle again. "Are you ever going to find a different way to announce your presence? Or are you insistent on becoming the office's own Cheshire Cat?"

"Yes." They laughed.

Etta paused, raising her eyebrows. "Yes, you're going to find a different way to announce your presence? Or yes, you insist on scaring the shit out of everybody all the time?"

"No," Cane replied.

Her face went slack, settling into a look of contempt. "You're ridiculous," she groaned.

"And hungry. You ready?"

Etta grabbed her scarf and jacket before following Cane to the parking lot.

Conversation wasn't a difficult task with Cane. It was as simple as them starting on a topic, and Etta commenting along or asking questions. Then those comments would result in Etta experiencing and sharing a memory or anecdote, and Cane would respond. There was no science, no nuances, no tricks or ulterior motives. It was just conversation.

"I'm still a little skeptical about last night," Cane mentioned, climbing into their car.

Etta paused, staring blankly at Cane. "How?" she whispered. "Burlesque dancers literally strutted out of *Vox Libri* and into your living room."

Cane rolled their hand out as if it was a full statement. "Exactly."

Etta settled into the car, confused and disheartened. They'd witnessed the scene together. The lights in Cane's apartment dimmed. A spotlight struck the corner and a tuxedo-clad dandy appeared. For fucks sake, she flew! And now Cane was doubting it all.

"Etta?"

"How would you explain it then? Collective insanity?"

Cane nodded with caution. "I mean, clearly I'm open to trying again and seeing what happens."

The two pulled into the restaurant, and Etta hopped out of the car in a huff. Cane reached into the backseat and pulled out *Vox Libri*.

"We're not gonna read it while we eat. Are we?" Etta asked, a sludge of nerves building up in her stomach. She knew how *Vox Libri* made her feel, but she had no idea how it made her look. While she flew across the sky that first time at The Attic, what was happening outside of her head? Was she sitting in her chair peacefully? Or were her motor functions still intact? When she and Cane watched the burlesque show, were they pools of lifeless bodies puddled on the couch, or attentive spectators watching an invisible extravaganza?

"Oh god, no—especially if I'm wrong," Cane reacted, and Etta felt herself relax. "I just like looking at it. It's nice to have by my side."

The place was small but packed. An ornate, gold-plated statue stood near the host stand, a strand of marigolds hanging around its neck. Paper lanterns hovered above every table and elegantly painted ceramic vases adorned the half-wall.

"How many?" a hostess asked before making her way to her station. Gesturing toward the two of them, the hostess interrupted Cane before they could speak. "Fifty-minute wait."

Cane turned to Etta with a grimace on their face. "That's a long time."

"I don't mind waiting." Etta shrugged.

Cane turned back to the hostess. "How long for take-out?"

"About fifteen to twenty minutes."

"Do you want to just get food to go?" Cane suggested. "We can take the food back to my place and give it another try?"

"Okay," Etta responded, the ends of her nerves igniting. The two placed their orders, grabbed the bags, and headed back to the car.

CHAPTER 13

——

Vox Libri lay across Etta's lap, shifting whenever Cane drove over a bump. Studying the gold embossing, she traced the relief pattern with her fingertips. She imagined the book-binder outlining the book dimensions onto the bare leather with a pencil before cutting it to size. He'd stain the material with dye made from vegetables before pasting it to the board. Then he'd overlay gold leaf, sealing it with egg whites and a heated, metal stamp, forever branding the book's flesh.

"Hey," Cane broke the silence, "so I noticed something yesterday."

Etta tore her gaze away from the book. Uneasily, she ushered Cane to continue.

"When we were in the coffee shop, you became—to put this as tactlessly as possible—a little manic there for a bit."

Etta felt herself tense up. "Well, yeah," she carefully began. "You saw the freaking Vaudevillian display that erupted from the book and into your living room. Could you imagine the reaction if that broke out in public?"

Cane's focus on the road intensified. "That's not when I'm talking about…"

Cane sat taller in their seat, their grip tightening on the steering wheel. They'd already told her they weren't convinced *Vox Libri* caused the shared illusion. What else was there to bring up?

"I meant when you were sharing your roommate's opinion on Dorian," Cane continued. "I believe the word you used was 'hermit'? I feel like I may have touched a nerve?"

Etta squeezed her eyes as tightly as they would close, the beginnings of a migraine probing its way through her temple. Her stomach hardened. Etta's ribcage constricted her lungs, and she couldn't move. She could only stare ahead, barely able to make out the naked silhouettes of trees in the dark. She rolled her neck and cracked her fingers to relieve whatever physical strain she could. Taking in a full breath, Etta shared Sam's comments on Dorian's sad existence. "He's concerned I'll end up just as lonely and crotchety."

Silence filled the car, the void swelling Etta's ears like someone shoving a bellow in both ears and forcing air into the canals. Each passing moment made her ears inflate, the pressure expanding to the brink of explosion. But just as they were about to burst, they pulled up to the apartment.

Cane put the car in park, exhaled, and then turned to Etta. "Ya know, Sam's not entirely wrong."

Etta hung her head. The person she'd just devoted time and energy to building a relationship with in an effort to prove Sam—and herself—wrong, agreed with Sam. It became clear. Destiny wanted her to be a lonely hermit, haunting the stacks of The Attic with no real accomplishments or relationships to show otherwise.

Hastily grabbing her by the shoulder, Cane continued, "That's not exactly what I meant!" Etta could hear the apology in their tone. "I mean, yeah, it's totally possible you'll end up like Dorian. But only if you let it happen."

She looked doubtfully over her shoulder at her consoler, curious with tears still welling up. Etta knew her future. Sam knew it. Any tarot cards she pulled told her so. Seconds earlier, even Cane said as much. Now they were backtracking, only to make Etta feel better. They were trying to save the night.

"Inaction is still an action. Right?" Cane explained, their hand leaving Etta's shoulder to instead grab her hand. "It's still a choice. But if you choose to do something—really anything—your future, your reality, changes."

Blinking hard, tears rolled down her cheeks. Etta chuckled, relief setting in. Cane had a point. And thinking it over, it wasn't far off from Sam's advice. So long as Etta made choices outside of spend-all-your-time-at-The-Attic, her doom would no longer be impending.

"Bottom line," Cane continued, "just choose not to end up that way. Ya know?"

Etta felt the corners of her mouth pull into a smile. The pressure in her head and ears began to subside like someone poking a hole in a balloon, letting the air slowly whistle out. She nodded and took a sharp breath in, pushing away any negative, sad thoughts that remained. She looked over at her friend who was also smiling and still holding her hand. Cane gave it a quick squeeze and a shake as if asking Etta to loosen up. The stress wasn't worth it. And they were right. Etta was full of choices. Northampton was the perfect example. Sure, it was impulsive, but it was still a life-changing decision—one that landed her with a job she didn't hate, a great roommate, a comfort zone, and a brilliantly unanticipated what-if.

She looked again at her latest decision, who sat back with a soft half-smile. Cane squeezed her hand again, quieting the last of Etta's worries. With a smug smirk, they pecked her hand before resting their chin on it.

"Food?"

"Food," Etta agreed, her insides soft and gooey. She let go of Cane's hand, hugged *Vox Libri* to her chest, and pushed the car door open. She walked over to the other side of the car and linked her free arm with Cane's. Turning her head, Etta waited for Cane to look back at her.

"Thank you." She sighed, laying her head on Cane's shoulder. The pair clung to one another until reaching the back door.

Cane welcomed her inside. The condo felt starkly empty without the dancers although Etta noticed different tchotchkes and collectibles than last time. Pictures of Cane and their family were scattered across the living room—Polaroids taped to walls, framed on end tables, and a small stack resting on the coffee table. Etta walked around scanning them all as Cane brought the food into the kitchen. She stopped in front of the bookshelf, studying the framed photo of a much younger, buzz-cut Cane standing next to a too-thin man being devoured by Cane's jacket.

"We took that about a year before he passed," Cane stated.

Etta turned to see them holding their now plated dinner. They gestured toward the table in the corner and then sat. Etta followed closely behind.

"Were you two close?" she asked, not necessarily knowing how to alleviate the uncomfortable tension that invariably followed the disclosure of a traumatic event.

Cane shrugged, their face unusually neutral. "I mean, it was contentious for sure. He loved us, but he also never hid the fact he wanted a son to be his mini-me. Instead, he got my two sisters and me. So surface level, the brunt of Little

League and Dad's garage helper was foisted on me. But my proclivity toward books and theater definitely confused him."

The pair awkwardly chuckled together and began eating. While mostly silent, Etta fixated on the fidgety Cane. Their bouncing leg sent a steady pulse that Etta could feel when resting her hand on the table. The subtle tremor traveled up her arm and settled high in her chest, constricting her breathing. As the minutes lurched forward, Cane's face became less aloof and more strained.

Etta's panicky brain made it difficult to come up with any talking points to veer away from the bubble of tension engulfing the pair. Shoveling another bite in her mouth, she looked over at *Vox Libri* sitting on the coffee table. She'd do anything to alleviate the antsy feeling and be as happy as she was both flying and watching the dancers in Cane's living room. Nearly jumping to her feet, Etta grabbed Cane's hand and dragged them to the couch. Pulling *Vox Libri* onto her lap, she smiled at Cane.

"Ready to be proven wrong?" Etta teased, leaning into Cane who rested their head on her shoulder. Closing her eyes, she settled the spine of the book on her knee and opened to a random page.

With his idea, I saw the sky—dark and green, fraught and ominous. In the meadow, I sensed the danger. The exposure. He stood positive, I negative, together vulnerable. And charged. Under a roof, we're protected. Safe from cruel critics and myopic muckrakers who'd hurry to see us staked and wasted until nothing but ash remained. Yet here we willingly hang from the sky, inviting God to see us for who we are. To ask Him to judge us freely and make of us as He will.

Greedily, we await Him. Bound and bonded by ironclad devotion for the other. But the heavens are bleak and gray and crack brightly under a thund'rous roar as His word is delivered.

They fell, the base of their heads resting on the back of the couch. The sound of metal gears on a track grinding against each other croaked from overhead. Looking upward, they noticed the ceiling rotating. Slowly, piece by piece, it began to unfurl like an opening eye.

Above them, they saw the sky. It was ominous and bleak with splotches of unsettling yellows like a healing bruise against one's flesh. The rumbling of the gears grew deeper, slowly becoming claps of thunder. As the ceiling opened up entirely, time seemed to slow and the air became charged. The static spread, raising the hair on their heads and arms. Currents rippled underneath their skin.

A bright light erupted from the dark atmosphere, cracking into a slow-moving bolt of lightning. Forcing and splitting itself across the scene, the electricity revealed the invisible veins of the sky. Etta and Cane, equally terrified and intrigued, followed the trails of the glowing circulatory system with their eyes. Each turn unveiled a new arm of sprouted branches; some thicker, some thin and frail.

Thunder rolled, loud and steady, like a symphony of kettle drums. Another crack of lightning pierced through the center of the sky. A solid ball of white light burned bright until it took the shape of a heart. Sinewy and muscular, but pure and untouched, it hovered above them and grew a steady pulse. The couple stared, mesmerized. It beat along to the rhythmic choir of thunder, growing brighter as the song crescendoed.

The heat from the storm melted away the remaining walls, trinkets, and pieces of furniture from Cane's apartment.

Within moments, Etta and Cane were standing in a grassy field as the storm raged around them. Adrenaline drumming throughout her body, Etta's uncertainty grew. Terrified of being struck, she withdrew into Cane's arms, and they wrapped her up tightly.

She looked up and saw sparks crackling in Cane's eyes and felt a charged stirring behind hers. Her own heart felt magnetized, pulling itself closer toward Cane. Etta began to feel more of her body pushing itself into Cane's. She looked down at her feet, seeing a thin strand decorated with brass keys entwining the couple and tightening the bond. It snaked its way up their bodies; encircling their thighs, hips, chests, and shoulders. As it writhed upward, the end tied itself to a kite and soared above. Just as the cord wrapped around their heads, about to press their lips together, another bolt of lightning cracked, striking the kite. Its current rocked throughout the coil. The blistering energy split the entangled, blasting them apart.

CHAPTER 14

———

The sun broke through the blinds, disturbing the night still behind her eyes. Etta kept them closed, squeezing them tighter to push the light away. Negotiating with the day, she asked for a few more minutes of sleep, but the morning had never been this relentless before. The tree outside her bedroom window usually did a much better job of keeping the sun away. Etta wondered what was so different about today for it to be so insistent.

As she opened her eyes, everything was still much brighter than she was used to. The sun bounced off a large mirror, reflected off of framed posters, and cast next to her resting head. Etta rolled away from the light. There, perfectly peaceful and still, lay Cane, fast asleep in their own bed.

Her stomach clenched, and her breathing stopped. Wired and confused, Etta wriggled from under the covers and carefully rolled off the bed. She landed in a crouch, feeling the brisk morning air against her bare skin. In a frenzy, Etta scanned the floor, picking up whatever clothing she recognized as she slipped into the hallway.

Closing the door behind her with the faintest of clicks, she tugged on her pants and pulled her shirt over her head. She took a moment to steady herself, trying to think over what happened the night before, but only images of sparks and lightning and a grassy field came to mind. The rest was fuzzy or entirely black. Panicked, she slapped around her body, blindly searching for her phone. Etta scurried into the kitchen and then the living room before spotting it on the coffee table next to *Vox Libri* lying open. She found her shoes, backpack, and jacket before rushing out the front door.

The morning sun felt brighter than usual and the sharp chill cut through to her spine. Shaking off the cold, Etta wished for nothing more than a pair of sunglasses as she bent down to tie her shoes. Throwing on her jacket, she unlocked her phone. Only an hour and a half before she had to be at work. From Cane's apartment to hers, the walk was at least fifty minutes, and then another twenty to Brain Train. That would leave twenty for her to shower, shove food into her mouth, and generally collect herself. But if she power-walked, or even jogged, she could shave some time off. Or she could call a cab and hope it'd arrived within minutes to give her some more time. And without another thought—other than being terrified of Cane finding her still on the stoop—Etta took off down the street, awkwardly waving to neighbors grabbing their morning papers.

Again, Etta thought back to the prior night. She remembered getting to Cane's. She remembered looking at their pictures and talking about their dad. They ate dinner, cracked open *Vox Libri*, and then ended up in a stormy meadow. Through the hallucination memory, Etta pictured glimpses of her and Cane. Like an astral projection, she watched the couple in her head, sitting on the couch deliriously out of their minds but blissful. They held on to each other tightly. At one point, Etta watched Cane lead the memory of her into their room, where they grasped at and for each other.

Etta reached her front door exhausted and out of breath. On the ever-growing list of things she couldn't remember, she added the last time she ran—recreationally or otherwise— and crossed off the previous night.

She trudged up the stairs toward her apartment and burst through the door. Cleese jumped and darted into Sam's room. Etta threw her keys at the wall, uncaring whether they landed on the table or bounced off the wall and onto the floor. She stopped short in the living room.

"Well, well," Sam began, his face stretching into the widest smile as he sat on the couch next to Riley, both ready for the day and enjoying their breakfast. "Good morning, Miss Dirty Stay-Out!"

"What an entrance!" Riley added, concealing his snicker behind a spoonful of cereal. Etta felt the warmth rise in her cheeks.

"And who do we have to blame for our dear Odette breaking curfew?" Sam trilled, posing the question to his partner.

Riley theatrically played along. "An army jacket, perhaps?"

Exasperated and still in a rush, Etta threw her backpack and coat on the empty section of the couch. "It is none of your business where I was last night," she grumbled and then hurried into her room.

"But, Etta," she heard Sam performatively call after her, "I was worried about you!"

"We thought you'd gone missing!" Riley's voice followed along with an eruption of cackling.

As she ripped fresh clothes from her closet and drawers, Sam and Riley were still teasing her from the other room.

"Doesn't she know Odette turns back into a swan after midnight?" and, "Cane must be into that sorta thing!" She desperately tried ignoring them, forcing herself to focus on the tasks at hand. Clothes. Towel. Shower. Coffee. Book it!

With an armful of her clothes, Etta reentered the living room and addressed the couple before fleeing into the bathroom. "You two are hilarious."

Etta tossed her things on top of the closed hamper and started the shower, hopping in regardless of the temperature. Even with her head under the falling water, she could still hear the ribbing from the other room, particularly the sing-song verses of "Etta's got a sweetheart... Etta's got a sweetheart!"

In less than an hour, Etta was supposed to see said sweetheart. But it was unclear if they'd remember anything about the night before. Or if they'd even believe it happened in the first place. Cane was already doubtful of *Vox Libri* and its charm. It was possible they'd be skeptical again. And if they were, Etta decided she'd make herself okay with it. Etta would have to be fine with not just maintaining their friendship but also coming to terms with her certain insanity. Hopefully, Cane was willing to come along for that ride at least.

Hopping out of the shower, she stared at herself in the steamed bathroom mirror. Etta hoped for the best then heard a knock at the door.

"All jokes aside," Sam said through the door, "there are lunch leftovers for you in the fridge. Riley and I are about to head to work. We can recap later. And be sure to put something more substantial than coffee in your body before you go!"

"Thank you." Etta sighed, listening for the front door.

She sat at her desk, dropping new words into her Scrabble game with Denise, and then refreshed her email. Etta had managed to slip into work without running into Cane, which she didn't mind. Regardless of Cane's reaction to the night before, Etta was not ready to hear it. Whatever the answer, it was bound to change the trajectory of their relationship. Whichever the response, all of Etta's work away from her hermit habits was now in peril.

Soon enough, the lunch hour approached. The now-or-never mentality edged its way into Etta's brain although the nerves still jostled her stomach. Realizing she hadn't seen any sight of Cane, Etta grew even more nervous. What if they never showed up to work? What if embarrassment over the night before or their resentment that Etta ran away in the morning made it so they couldn't bear to show their face?

Etta listened closely for any sign of Cane. She heard no clacking of keys coming from their cubicle. Or the sound of rolling chair wheels zipping back and forth as they played Cubicle Pong. It was just radio silence.

"Odette?"

She jerked in her chair, looking up to see Agnes peeking above the cubicle wall. "Valeska and I are going to the Olympic Deli again for a quick luncheon. Would you like to come along?"

"No, thank you, Agnes," Etta replied, trying desperately to settle herself and sound normal. "I brought leftovers today."

"Oh, how nice! Something Cleese made, perhaps?"

Etta's brain short-circuited, contorting her face in confusion before quickly realizing Agnes confused her roommate for the cat. Etta didn't feel like correcting her. "Uh, yep." She wanted nothing more than for this conversation to be over so she could check on Cane's attendance.

"What did he make this time?"

Reminding herself to be patient, Etta took a quick breath. Agnes was a harmless older woman with an intense need to exchange pleasantries. Besides Valeska, Etta was the only other person in the office congenial enough to hold longer conversations with her. Etta had lost count of the number of times she accidentally eavesdropped on Denise, Terach, and even Cane in the breakroom snickering about Agnes and her accent or over-eagerness to share stories.

"Last night," Etta began, "my roommate decided to teach his boyfriend how to make these traditional Lebanese meat pies called sfiha. They made a few extras and packed me some for lunch today."

"How sweet!" Agnes smiled, her cheeks reddening as she cast her gaze out. "I remember trying to show Bradley how to roll pretzels after our wedding. Flour, salt, sugar; that's all it takes, but *ach*. He was useless!"

Etta politely smiled as Agnes's hands rose in the air. "But my Thomas, he loved it. And now Tommy comes over to make pretzels with me. He tells me..." She scrunched up her face, making her voice mockingly nasally. "'*Oma*, it's like brown Play-Doh but you can eat it!'"

Out of the corner of her eye, Etta saw Cane walk past her cubicle and into the breakroom. Now very aware of her posture, she became eager for Agnes to wrap up the story. Cane did show up to work. Meaning that even if they did regret whatever happened or didn't happen the night before, it wasn't enough to prevent them from seeing Etta at work. Etta pushed away from her desk, hoping Agnes would take the hint.

"Cooking is such good, *hiya callit*, bonding," Agnes said, sentimentally nodding her head. Etta's mood perked, taking the *"hiya callit"* as a cosmic sign of good faith, and stood up from her desk. "But all right, I'll let you go. Enjoy your saf—saf-hat—, your meat pie."

Agnes disappeared beneath the cubicle wall as Etta scurried to the breakroom. Cane stood with their back to the door, leaning all of their weight on their hands and propping themselves against the counter. Etta nervously approached as the microwave faintly hummed in the background.

"Sorry for ditching you this morning," Etta began, gently at first until the nerves took over, gradually increasing her talking speed. "I didn't want to wake you and was worried about making it to work on time."

Cane remained with their back turned. The only acknowledgment was a slight shift of their head, barely turning enough to hear Etta better. But when Cane didn't reply, Etta's restless impatience urged her to keep speaking.

"Agnes was just at my cubicle," Etta continued. "She asked me if I wanted to go to lunch with her, but that's not the point. The point is she said it. She said *hiya callit!* Obviously, I had to tell you immediately."

Cane's head sank lower until it hid beneath their shoulders. Etta could see their grip tighten on the edge of the counter. Cane let out an audible sigh but still didn't reply.

"I…" Etta stammered, the concern growing in her voice. "Is everything okay? What happened?"

The bell of the microwave rang. Cane slowly corrected their posture, pulled open the door, and grabbed their food. They turned, making cold eye contact with Etta before taking a seat at the table. Cane's brow furrowed as they pushed their food around with the fork. Then Cane let it fall, plastic hitting plastic.

"It's too hot to eat," Cane murmured.

Etta walked closer to the table, reaching out to place her hand on Cane's shoulder. "Do you want to talk? Is it about last night?"

In the distance, the pair could hear Denise and Terach chattering. Cane's features tightened as they looked at Etta. Cane stood up, grabbing their Tupperware.

"Something else. And yes, but not here." Cane pushed their chair under the table. "Grab your food first, but—my cubicle."

"I'm not hungry yet," Etta quickly replied, urging Cane out of the breakroom.

Making their way toward Cane's cubicle, Etta looked around, taking inventory of who was left in the office. They said it had nothing to do with last night, but regardless, Etta wasn't interested in generating any office romance rumors today. Besides, whatever was upsetting Cane, Etta was positive they didn't want it announced to their coworkers either. If Terach left the breakroom, he was probably at his desk with his comically giant headphones on, listening to some NPR podcast. And Denise would have moved to sit in the common area with another lady from the HR department for as long as she could get away with it.

Cane tossed their lunch with too much force. The fork tumbled out, scattering noodles, cheese, and olive oil across the desk. They swore loudly, causing Etta to jump, and then threw themself into their chair. Cane's head hung off the back as they massaged their forehead with the heel of their hand.

Standing just inside the cubicle, Etta caught a glimpse of an obituary pulled up on the computer. Paired with the piece was a cropped photo of a man in his early thirties, smiling at the camera, a beautiful landscape over his shoulder. Etta stepped closer, leaning in to read about Scott Greer, beloved husband and father of two, age thirty-four, who unexpectedly passed away late last week. He worked as a biology teacher at his alma mater, Enfield High School in Connecticut, and graduated from UMASS in 2003. Scott is survived by his wife, Kathy, and Alexander, age four, and Jeremy, age two. A memorial is planned for at Browne Memorial on Sunday.

"Who was he?" Etta gently asked.

Cane sat up straight, staring at the computer screen. "Some guy I knew a lifetime ago."

"Were you two close?"

Cane scoffed. "Not really. We went to the same high school, but he was a few years older. He dated my girlfriend's sister, so he was around. He'd take us out for ice cream sometimes and was just a nice guy. Always burning mixed CDs for Ally that Jenna and I would steal. Lots of Strokes and The Shins."

"How'd...?"

"My sister sent me the link this morning. He wasn't even sick. He was on vacation with his family. It was a horrific surfing accident. Can you imagine? His poor fucking family. One minute, they're having a grand ol' time. The next, he's washing up to shore," Cane explained. "Apparently, he was on life support for weeks. Then they just pulled the plug."

Cane's face tightened. Their distress was apparent. But while Cane wasn't mourning a lost acquaintance, it became clear they were mourning the loss of their own lost lifetime. The one spent in the backseat of Scott's car, holding hands with Jenna as they sang along to the stereo on their way to something simpler than adulthood. Etta thought back to her own past self and the players involved and felt the persistent fog of grief cloud her mind.

"Are you gonna go home to the funeral?" Etta asked.

"What? No. That'd be weird."

"Why? Just go and pay your respects. Get some closure."

"Because I haven't talked to the guy in like sixteen years. Like absolutely no contact."

"You can just go and sit in the back corner. You don't need to make a big deal of it."

"No," Cane punctuated. "I don't know his wife, and I never met his parents. That's fucking weird."

"Okay."

"Okay."

Etta didn't know how to proceed. Of course, Cane was hurt, so they deserved patience. But they'd never been short with Etta before. At least not like this. Etta felt her insides turn to a billion skittering bugs between the layers of skin and bone. More than anything, she wanted to rip open a hole and scoop them all out. Then she'd run to Cane's apartment, grab *Vox Libri*, and disappear into a more fantastical world. Anything to escape this purgatorial moment.

Etta admonished herself for being so sensitive. It wasn't that big of a deal. Cane needed support. They needed Etta in this moment. She could put aside her own internal hang-ups over tone aside and push through her own discomfort. So Etta composed herself.

"Do you wanna take a walk or something?" Etta asked, unsure of what to do and feeling somehow responsible for making Cane feel better.

"What? No. I'm fine." Cane brushed off the suggestion, turning their chair away to face the computer and closing the obituary. "I'll be fine. I'm just... Fuck. You know?"

CHAPTER 15

The day passed by without another word from Cane. No mention of the night before. No discussion of what happened next. And Etta understood. How could she expect Cane to think about anything else while they were mourning the passing of a friend? She couldn't let her own anxieties and worry get in the way. Because that'd be selfish. But when she came home to an empty apartment, she couldn't brush off the heavy feeling in her stomach of wanting to unload.

Etta threw her backpack on the floor and settled on the corner of her bed, acutely aware that wasn't where she slept the night before. Her untouched covers remained twisted and unkempt, just as she'd left them before leaving for work yesterday morning. Although nothing had changed—enough time hadn't passed for anything to change—she felt similarly to when she'd visit home and walk into her childhood bedroom. Like walking into a time capsule. A room frozen in a forgotten lifetime.

Unnerved, Etta shot up from her bed and ran to her closet. She needed an escape, but *Vox Libri* was at Cane's. And at the moment, she didn't know where they stood. Nor did she want to bother Cane right now. Etta suspected they weren't in a proper headspace to experience whatever *Vox Libri* did. So instead, she would go to The Attic.

She ripped off her work clothes, threw on jeans and a t-shirt, and shoved her notebook into her backpack. Etta heard the front door close and keys crash on the end table followed by Sam's muffled voice cooing at Cleese. She threw her hair up into a poor excuse of a ballet bun and began layering up to leave. Her progress was interrupted by a knock. Turning toward the sound, Etta saw Sam standing in the doorway cradling Cleese like a newborn.

"Welcome home, stranger," he teased. "Is that an overnight bag I see? Thought you'd sneak away again before explaining yourself?"

"I'm going to The Attic," Etta replied plainly, tossing her backpack onto the bed. The rant boiled inside her like a kettle on the stove. She felt it rising from the bottom of her stomach to the base of her esophagus, ready to whistle. But just as she opened her mouth to let the tea pour, Sam spoke.

"If you have a partner now, why go back to that place?"

Etta froze. Partner? She'd only just recently started calling Cane a friend. And she wasn't entirely positive about what happened the night before. She couldn't remember. But regardless, why would having or not having a partner affect Etta spending time at The Attic? If she did have a partner or even just a friend, that would leave less time to spend with Dorian among the books—which was what Sam wanted and even suggested—but that wouldn't stop the visits entirely.

"Because I like it there," Etta defended.

"Okay, touchy."

Etta glared at Sam as she zipped up her backpack. She couldn't deal with another person lacking tone control. Not when she couldn't control her own.

"Excuse me," she said, stepping directly in front of Sam as he blocked the door. He moved aside, but she could feel her bag graze his arm.

"Sorry for being excited for you," Sam called out behind her, forcing Etta to pause and turn toward her roommate. Swallowing her agitation, she mustered up any remaining patience and waited for Sam to continue. "It was nice to see you creating a life for yourself is all. Ya know, giving yourself a chance at happiness or whatever."

As hard as she tried, Etta still rolled her eyes but softened otherwise. The tone soured the sweet sentiment, but Etta appreciated it anyway. With her hand on the doorknob, she whispered a thank you before darting out the door.

Etta moseyed down the street toward The Attic. Her breath was short, and she blamed it on wrapping her scarf too tightly, actively ignoring her erratic breathing throughout the day. Her last visit to The Attic was tense. And she wasn't alone. And it didn't end well. Etta had seen Dorian upset before but never at her. Or at least not in that way. So she expected things to be unusual, but she needed an escape—somewhere quiet to distract herself from the mess of the day.

The door seemed heavier somehow as she pushed it open. She turned to walk behind the front desk and jumped. Dorian stood there, a book in his hand under the small lamp sitting next to the register. He wasn't upstairs like he usually was. Instead, Dorian stood glancing at Etta above the glasses hanging from the tip of his nose.

"Hi," Etta greeted him, still startled, trying to slow her breathing down.

"Hello," Dorian replied. He pushed his glasses to the top of his head, slicking his hair back in the process and then bookmarking his page.

Etta timidly walked over to the armoire behind the desk and opened the door, very aware of Dorian's presence. She dropped her backpack on the floor and grabbed a hanger to put her jacket away. She closed the door quietly behind her and noticed Dorian heading toward his office.

"How've you been?" she quickly asked before he could make his way up the stairs. Dorian pivoted slowly, taking his glasses off the top of his head and ruffling his hair before rubbing his eyes and then putting them back.

"No different than usual," he replied. Etta noted Dorian looked the most sleep-deprived she'd ever seen him.

The Attic fell silent. Usually, the silence was comforting—relaxing almost—but this was different. The air was thick, suspending the visible dust particles and making them seem more still than usual like the bits of fruit Etta's mother would add to the Jell-O molds she made every Christmas, Easter, and Thanksgiving.

"Have you been working on anything new?"

Etta felt the resistance from the silence as she spoke. It fought back, wanting to keep everything quiet so the tension would remain at bay. Still facing Etta, Dorian took a step up.

"No," he said. "But I've made some slow progress on the restoration project."

"That's good!" Her voice jumped an inappropriate number of octaves. "Slow progress is still progress. Right?"

"Mm-hmm," Dorian replied as he committed to making his way up the stairs.

"Maybe I can see how far along you are later?" Etta called.

"Sure." Dorian continued up the stairs without turning around.

Etta heard the door to his office close. She picked up her backpack and laid it on the counter. Her breathing was still shallow, growing more and more rapid. She couldn't have been that out of shape. Her sprint this morning proved otherwise. Trying to take a stabilizing breath, Etta lay her hands on the flat surface of the desk, hoping to ground herself. But then she took another inhale then another and another. Grabbing the stool Dorian had been sitting on, she perched on the edge. Remembering an old trick her mother taught her, Etta placed her hands on her hips and straightened her spine, opening up her chest as widely as possible to allow more air in. Eventually, the air became less thick. The dust particles again moved at their leisurely pace. And she could control her breathing.

Her mind meandered. Dorian was sitting alone in his office. But he always sat alone in his office. However, he wasn't always angry with her and sitting alone in his office. And her stomach started to turn.

She grabbed her backpack and walked to her usual table, completely aware of every sound she made. As quiet as Etta's steps were, she sounded like an elephant wearing high-heeled shoes walking up a flight of stairs made of wood in a hollow cave. Or at least that's how it sounded to her.

She took a seat at her table. The chair scraped against the floor and creaked under her weight. She unzipped her backpack and felt the echo bouncing off the bookshelves. She pulled her notebook from her backpack and carefully laid it on the desk. The pages flopped and wobbled when she opened the notebook and the rings scratched against the table when she pushed it to the side.

Etta took another deep breath. No way was she being as loud as she felt. It just wasn't possible. And besides, Dorian was upstairs and his door was closed. So even if she was being loud, he probably wouldn't hear her.

She popped her headphones into her ears to drown out her own sounds. A song from Cabaret played and Etta closed her eyes. Slowly, her mind wandered back to the burlesque show in Cane's apartment. The colors were duller and the visuals were fuzzy, but they were there. And loud. Everything was still so loud. Her brain couldn't finish a thought. Etta couldn't complete a single visual. The pieces and pictures jumped from the woman at her vanity to the web of lightning, back to the fringed skirts of burlesque dancers, and then the open skies. The wind picked up speed, and Etta was quickly swept up in a tornado. Like Dorothy, the funnel filled with the characters from *Vox Libri*, swirling around her until she flew up through the anvil and then catapulted toward the ground.

Etta pulled her headphones out moments before impact and stopped herself from shrieking. Then the lights turned out, leaving only the desk lamp lit. Unnerved, she tried looking through the darkness.

"Dorian?" Etta called out, unsure whether she was still daydreaming. Everything remained grimly still before the lights turned back on. She quickly collected her things, shoving them into her backpack, and shuffled to the front of the shop. Spotting something in the corner of her eye, Etta yelped. Dorian stood by the stairs.

"I didn't realize you were still here."

She looked at his expressionless face as he leaned against the staircase. His glasses were on and his hair frayed everywhere. He grabbed the pack of cigarettes from his cardigan pocket, pulled one out, and then tucked it behind his ear.

"I always stay until close," Etta replied, throwing her backpack over her shoulder. Her heart shuddered as if she'd been electric shocked and she was experiencing after effects. Even her hands on her hips couldn't help slow her breathing down this time.

"Yeah, well, you didn't last time," Dorian said turning toward the door. Another person with a tone. Etta followed behind him but walked out silently. Although exhausted, she was also desperate. She couldn't leave on another bad note. The Attic was her first safe space after moving to Massachusetts. Losing that wasn't an option. And since Dorian wasn't going to make the effort, she knew she had to.

"*Vox Libri* is so much more fascinating than I could've imagined," Etta said. The two stood outside of the storefront as Dorian locked up and lit a cigarette. She hated small talk, but she had to try. "Cane and I have been tearing through it nonstop."

Dorian blew out smoke and nodded along.

Etta fell quiet for a moment. She had one last fall back. "I mean... The way Ms. Fairfax remembers it from her childhood might be more accurate than she realizes."

Dorian kept nodding, clearly not listening, and then headed toward the parking lot with Etta following slowly. He opened his car door and started to climb inside.

"Hey, Dorian," Etta said, stopping him before he closed it. "I'm sorry for the way Cane and I left last time. I'm not entirely sure what happened between the two of you, but I don't really know why you're upset with me."

"I'm not upset with you," he replied before shutting the door behind him.

Etta backed up as the engine started. She could feel her insides hollowing out as she watched Dorian pull away.

CHAPTER 16

———

Etta sat cross-legged on the bed, the pillows propping up her back. Cane walked into the room holding *Vox Libri*. They laid it across Etta's lap and took a seat, their thighs touching hers. Opening the book, Etta read aloud about the passage of time and its tendency to move at both rapid and glacial speeds. The couple braced themselves, waiting for the next spectacle to begin. Their eyes darted from one corner of the room to the next. They listened for any unusual sounds. They watched for the slightest hint of peculiar movement or strange transformations around them.

"Why isn't it working?" The disappointment poisoned Cane's voice. Etta watched as their face grew harder. Wrapping her arms around Cane, Etta burrowed her head in their neck. She felt Cane let go as their body melted into Etta's. She let her own body relax and the pair sank deeper into the bed.

Turning in toward each other, Etta watched as Cane struggled to hold back tears. She understood Cane was mourning the death of their friend, but she couldn't find a moment from her own past where she could relate. She'd never experienced loss like this in her own life. For a moment,

Etta imagined she was being hooked up to an IV injecting a jittery combination of gratitude and guilt through her veins. She traced her own arm with her fingertips until she reached a catheter in the crook of her elbow.

Panicked, Etta looked across the bed. Cane lay there, unaware of the gauze and rubber tubing now sticking out of Etta's arm. The lights abruptly dimmed and swiftly brightened. Then they did it again and once more before totally blackening. Scuttling her free hand around the bed, Etta searched for any sign of Cane to no avail. She was alone.

Etta rolled onto her back, the alarm surging from the drip and circulating throughout her body. Her chest felt heavy, and she was unable to sit up. A whirring sound ticked next to her like a baseball card pinned to the spokes of a bike wheel. Etta turned her head—the only bit of herself she could currently move—toward the sound. A faint silver gleam dilated from a tunnel. Growing brighter, the light revealed an old movie projector with film reels locked and loaded.

The cone of light grew wider and wider, reaching the opposite wall of Cane's bedroom. It projected giant numbers, counting backward from five before a jaunty ragtime tune played over a black and white title card reading *The Life and Death of Odette Colby* before flashing to another.

I. Birth

The music faded into another song, a familiar sound—soft and sweet and soothing, bows rubbing against the lilting strings of violins and violas.

A woman appeared on the screen, her back to the camera. Her pastel striped polo was tucked in deep to her belted high-waisted jeans cuffed just enough to rest on her starchy Keds. She looked over her shoulder smiling at the camera. The woman looked familiar, but Etta couldn't suss out where she knew her from. So she lay there mesmerized, studying the thick, brightly colored headband pushing back the woman's fluffy hair.

As a cello joined the orchestra, cradling the melody of the unforgettable lullaby, the camera slowly revolved around the woman. In her arms lay a newborn swaddled in a knitted blanket. The baby, her eyes unopened, stretched out an arm toward her mother's face. The woman's warm smile shifted into pursed lips affectionately kissing the baby's palm. Then the screen and song faded to a closeup of the baby's face.

The bright piano pealed its syncopated opening, the next title card appearing over the baby's head as the film fast-forwarded through time, aging her up to a young girl.

II. Childhood

Her light brown hair matched the woman's from the last scene, but her curls hung loosely around her shoulders. The girl's cheeks plumped as she cheesed for the camera, and Etta finally recognized herself.

The young girl scampered off to the scene behind her, Etta's childhood backyard. The summer sun was high as a sprinkler fanned and waved at least six feet overhead. Young Etta, in her rainbow bathing suit, raced back and forth giggling as she hopped and skipped through the spurting water. In the background, Etta could see her parents and sister. They looked younger than when she saw them last; her father at the grill with his longer hair gelled back, and the woman from the previous scene with a toddler on her hip. Young Etta tripped over the sprinkler, landing face first in the grass. She lifted her head to scream as blood crusted around her nose.

The camera moved in to a close-up of Young Etta sitting criss-cross-applesauce with the sprinkler behind her. Cupping the tiniest tooth in her hands, she poked her tongue through the new hole in her mouth, and the music changed again to a slow, plucky waltz. Again, Young Etta aged and text appeared above her head.

III. Adolescence

Teenage Etta's hair was flat-iron straight, her teeth behind turquoise-banded braces, and she layered her yellow polo with a peacock blue one on top.

Etta watched her younger self walk out of her old high school, past group after group of other kids her age. Clutching her oversized binder, Young Etta hung her head, avoiding eye contact with anyone who passed her. After finally finding a secluded place to sit, she pulled a battered notebook and dictionary from her backpack. The camera angled to the notebook and focused in on a scribbled word map.

IV. Adulthood—the state or period of being fully grown, fully developed, or of age—a blend of the Latin *adultus* meaning "grown" and the Middle English suffix -*hod* denoting a state or condition.

The picture pulled away revealing Etta sitting at her work desk. She was fully grown. The same age as she currently was.

Etta dropped her eyes, making sure she was still lying in the bed and not actually at Brain Train.

Other Etta rose from her seat, picking up all of her belongings. She looked down at her doppelganger's feet, noticing a moving walkway. As Other Etta walked along, the Brain Train scenery split into three separate pieces behind her, smoothly rotating to reveal her apartment. In the background, Sam and Riley sat on the couch with Cleese in their lap. Etta tossed her backpack toward them before the setting divided again, displaying The Attic.

Stepping off the walkway, Etta took a seat in her usual spot. The camera positioned itself to look her directly in the eyes. Then as if on a timelapse, The Attic remained still but Etta watch her other self age. Her hair grayed. Her laugh lines grew deeper. Her eyes became duller and duller until the picture faded to black.

V. End

The film stopped. The room was black. It was quiet. Etta reached for her arm but could no longer feel any gauze or tubes. Frantically, she wriggled each of her limbs. Realizing she was no longer weighted down, she rolled back to her side and reached across the bed. She found Cane's face in the darkness and held it in her hands. Their cheeks were wet, and Etta could hear a faint sniffling. Etta pulled Cane closer, fiercely kissing them until they were both out of breath.

After hours of angst, dread, and utter turmoil, Etta found a moment of clarity. She hadn't felt this tumultuous in almost a year. And her last lucid moment brought her to Northampton.

As she pulled away, Etta could make out Cane's silhouette now that her eyes had adjusted to the darkness. Cane looked back at her, their face in a sad but gentle smile. Etta played with Cane's hair, pushing the short strands out of their face. "Let's get out of here."

INTERLUDE

——

You've been sitting on the dirt path for quite some time. Enough that it shows on your face. Mud has dried across your cheeks. Twigs and leaves are stuck in your hair. Dirt is caked under your fingernails. Your clothes are torn at the edges from getting caught on branches.

You've lost track of how long it's been since you've seen your friends. So many ants, mice, owls, and deer have passed by that you've stopped counting. The trees feel like they've grown denser and the path behind looks more overgrown than ever. The lack of sun makes you and the forest cold. You feel frozen in more ways than one. You have no way to turn around in the thickets and thorns. No way to go back to find any of the forks your friends took.

You think of your friends always. You remember the jokes, the stories, the talks of your adventures ahead. You miss the hopping, skipping, running, and dancing. But most of all, you miss the company. You long for the days when everything was well. Everything was good. And you begin to cry.

The tears start small—a sniffle here, a droplet there. But once the levee breaks, there's no stopping the flood. It's overwhelming and difficult to breathe. You're wet and frustrated. You feel lonely and betrayed, forgotten and abandoned. You're terrified of the unknown—of forging ahead. But you also know there's no turning back.

So, you have two options—continue sitting in the middle of an overgrown dirt path and wallow or stand up, dust off the dirt, dry your face, and begin walking again.

The path ahead is overgrown but less so than the path behind. The path ahead is also dark, but still less than where you came. There's no knowing what lies on the path ahead, but you figure it's better than nothing. If your friends did it, so can you. They were just as anxious, restless, excited, and curious as you are now. It only took you a little longer to get there. You let these emotions get the better of you and decide to continue on.

As you walk down the crowded path, taking careful steps to avoid tripping over a rock, falling into a thorny bush, or getting scratched by a low-hanging branch, you wonder whether your friends had as many obstacles. Had you followed them down one of their trails, would you have had an easier time? A piece of you knows the answer doesn't matter. This is the path you're on now, and there's no changing it. This is the hand you've dealt yourself.

The longer you push forward, the easier the journey seems to get. It's unclear whether there are fewer brambles or you've just grown stronger. Regardless, now you notice the sun breaking through the leaves more often. It's unclear whether the sun is better at warming the earth or all the hiking has warmed your bones. Either way, your journey feels more peaceful.

Eventually, you come to a new fork in the road. Both paths are equally shaded. Both paths are the same width.

Both paths have the same number of trees. Neither path has a directional sign. You rack your brain for what to do.

You can continue down the same path you always have. You know there will probably be more trees and shade and underbrush, but you're more resilient now than ever.

You can choose to take the new path and head into the unknown. You don't know what's ahead, but there could be fewer trees and more sun and it could be clearer. But that's all speculation.

You can't help but resent your friends. When they were confronted with a similar decision, they had someone to discuss options with. But you're alone. The decision is entirely up to you. And you feel paralyzed.

While the outside is frozen, your insides are shaking with small twitches and cringes at first and then growing to full-on convulsions. The soft forest sounds feel like they're blasting through a stadium speaker. The small bits of sun peeking through the trees are blindingly bright. Your hands fly up to your head, you close your eyes tightly, and you crouch down in an attempt to block everything out and make it all quiet.

With your chin resting on your knees, you notice a rock lying at the edge of the path, sitting right at the point where the trail splits. It's flat and small, no larger than a dime. If there were a lake around, it'd be the perfect skipping stone. You pick it up. The surface is soft and smooth so you push it around your hand, weaving it in and out of your fingers. The fidgeting helps quiet your brain.

As you turn it around in your hand, you notice a white stripe running down the opposite side. An idea strikes. Gray on one side, stripe on the other. You can flip the rock like a coin. You can assign the left path to the gray, and the right path to the stripe.

The anticipation builds in your stomach. A decision will be made. You will find an answer. You will take one of these paths. Instead of letting opportunity pass you by; instead of letting uncertainty get the better of you; instead of sitting in the dirt waiting for nothing, your journey will continue.

The buzz of adventure rings through the air. The frenzy of impulse makes your head spin. The warmth of certainty blankets your shoulders and you toss the rock above your head.

You watch as it twirls in slow motion. As it reaches the peak of the flop, it hangs there as if it's hung from the sky by a string. Gravity is perverse. She knows how much it's taken for you to get to this moment, and still, she chooses to tease you. She needs to know you will appreciate the coming relief.

Just as the rock is about to fall back to the ground—just before you're going to get your answer—a bird swoops overhead. The bird snatches it and flies down one of the paths.

You've waited far too long to get your answer. You need to know the result. You chase after the bird.

CHAPTER 17

———

Nothing could've prepared Etta for the darkness. For the unknown looming just outside of their headlights—nothing else before them but the road. Nothing prepared her for the behemoths she could barely make out along the edge of the shadows, almost like the guardians of their final destination. But least of all, nothing prepared her for the uneasiness stirring in her gut as she half-expected these giants to lunge forward to make their attack.

But through the uncertainty and fear and exhaustion, Etta was ready to reach the gates of heaven.

And they did.

The main entrance to the park was left unattended. The only thing greeting Etta and Cane was a sign urging all Zion visitors to turn on their high beams and be cautious of the mule deer. They migrate at night when it's quiet.

"Why'd you turn the music down?" Cane interjected as Etta settled back into the passenger seat.

"Our windows are down," she answered. "And people are asleep."

"Yeah, but they're probably dead asleep."

"You know the mountains actually amplify sound, right? Because of echoes. And tents are made of thin fabric that absorbs sound instead of deflecting it, right?"

Cane shrugged.

"It's almost two!" Etta laughed. "And I'd rather if our neighbors didn't hate us."

Cane let a hand off the steering wheel and the windows started to rise.

"No, wait!" Etta tried interjecting, her hand flying to the buttons on her side. "It's nice out."

"You're impossible." She could feel the eye roll.

"I don't think it's ludicrous to keep the windows where they are and to turn the music down," Etta irritably continued.

She watched as much of the road as she could as Cane crept their way toward the campground. But through the darkness, all Etta could see were the few bushes, short trees, and mile markers lining the paved path.

"What's our campground letter again?" Cane asked passing the first campground sign.

"B."

"Okay," Cane said reaching for the radio knob. Etta swatted their hand away. She watched Cane's face pull into a tight-lipped grin as they pulled into the assigned campground. "What's the spot number?"

"28."

Cane stopped the van in front of the only brick structure around.

"Alright," they said switching off the ignition before turning to look at Etta. "Grab your toiletries. You're gonna want to use the bathroom now instead of having to walk here from our spot with a flashlight. Trust me."

Etta unclicked her seatbelt, opened her door, and then pulled the sliding door of the minivan open. Climbing into the back, across where the middle seats used to be, Etta pulled her toothbrush, face wipes, and pajamas out of her duffle and then climbed back out. Cane followed quickly behind walking toward the other stall.

Etta quickly readied herself for bed, using her phone as a flashlight to and from the restroom before hopping back into the passenger seat. She pulled out her phone hoping to text Sam to tell him not to worry because she was okay, but she didn't have any service. For which she was thankful. Because at least now the texts and calls from Valeska would stop.

"You can't be bored already," Cane said appearing in the window and making Etta jump. The last five days had exhausted her. Day in and out was nothing but driving, pausing only to eat and sleep. Etta shoved Cane's shoulder a little too hard and then watched them walk around the van, waiting to answer until they were back in the driver's seat.

"One, you're an ass," Etta replied, trying to lighten her own mood. "Two, I just wanted to let Sam know I have yet to be eaten by a wild coyote."

Cane chuckled, turning on the ignition. "I doubt the likelihood of that happening. Especially because we're only staying in park campgrounds with plenty of other people."

"Totally fair, but Sam has zero idea where I am. It's been days since I've seen him. The last we spoke, I was on my way to The Attic," she continued, ignoring Cane scoffing. Both had actively avoided mentioning Dorian. "Then I hopped into your bed, booked an impromptu flight, rented a minivan, and have basically been aimlessly driving through the desert ever since."

"Wasn't he the one who said you should be more adventurous? Less passive? Isn't this exactly that?"

Etta paused to reflect. Sam had expressed concern for Etta's unlived experiences. And here she was taking his advice. Or at least something close to his advice. She let the phone fall out of her hand and into her lap.

"How come you haven't gotten any calls or messages from Valeska? I feel like I've been getting them nonstop."

"I probably have, but I put my phone on *Do Not Disturb* at the airport. I absolutely do not feel like being disturbed." Cane laughed.

As the two continued toward their campsite, Etta felt like she was at an RV convention, seeing all the different sizes and styles of recreational vehicles available. They passed mansions on wheels, a teardrop trailer supplemented with a tent, Airstreams, and something that looked like it drove right off the set of *Breaking Bad*. Cane slowly pulled their minivan into an open spot and parked it.

"Alright, let's roll out the topper." They sighed before climbing into the back.

Etta watched Cane walk straight through where the missing seats were. Concerned about spending too much on hotels, Cane brought Etta to a car rental to pick up a minivan. The couple removed the middle seats before taking off, leaving them at the rental. Afterward, they stopped to pick up supplies. Up against the back bench was a rolled-up mattress pad about four inches thick, which Cane unfurled before covering it with a loose bedsheet. They reached across the back bench into the trunk and tossed Etta a backpack of more sheets. She unzipped the bag and fastened its contents to the ceiling, effectively shielding them from outside eyes.

"Okay, so, easy day tomorrow," Cane began, settling into the makeshift bed. "We'll sleep in a bit, grab breakfast at the café, do the Emerald Pools tomorrow, maybe relax by the river and then go to a ranger program? Tomorrow is supposed to be one about parasites, so that should be cool."

"Uh-huh," Etta involuntarily replied.

"I mean," Cane said uneasily, "unless you think you're ready to careen right into the Subway?"

Etta scoffed, finally paying attention. "What? No!"

Cane snickered.

"Definitely an easy day tomorrow. Please and thank you," she continued, thankful for the break from the fraught tension. "I know the hills in Northampton are rough, but I am *not* ready for that."

Through the starlight, Etta could see Cane smile as they lay on their back. Etta climbed into bed, pulling the sheets over her shoulder. She could spot Cane's silhouette through the night, their chest steadily rising and falling with each breath. Etta wondered what it would feel like to slide her arm across it and savor the rise and fall.

"Okay, so easy day tomorrow," Cane settled on, pulling the sheet over their shoulders and crossing their hands over their stomach. Etta exhaled as deeply and steadily as she could muster. "We can hike the Narrows on Wednesday. You bought extra layers. Right? We're gonna get wet and you'll want something warm and dry for afterward."

"Mm-hmm."

Cane pulled out their phone. Its glow illuminated the profile of their face, the only thing visible in the dark for Etta to see. She was starting to believe that no matter how many days they spent alone together, Etta would never know where she and Cane stood. Whether they were a couple or only seeing what happens. She tried to stay cool about it, but among the close quarters and lack of proper sleep, it was becoming increasingly difficult. Cane fumbled with something on the screen for a moment before setting it down.

"Alarms are set, and we're good to go."

Etta took a breath, settling the quaking she felt throughout her body.

"There's no way you're cold," Cane teased, throwing their own arm around Etta under the covers. She could feel Cane's body softening against her own. She envied Cane's ability to be so relaxed while she still couldn't get herself to do the same. As she fidgeted to find a comfortable position, Cane pulled her in tighter, kissing her temple. "I'm glad you're here with me right now."

Whatever uncertainty Etta held momentarily left her body. The warmth of Cane's words melted her insides. In that moment, she was also glad to be with Cane. She was happy to be alone with them to spend an indeterminate amount of uninterrupted time accompanied by scenic vistas in the background. *How picturesque*, she thought. *How fairy tale.*

"Me too," Etta whispered back.

"I was itching to get away," Cane continued. "I was restless. That nine to five, five day a week cycle was slowly eating away at me. It was driving me nuts."

"Really? I found it kinda comforting," Etta explained, thinking fondly of her walks to work and her quiet evenings at The Attic. Cane pulled away. Even in the dark, Etta could tell they were staring at her intensely. "What?"

"I mean… You always talk about how you don't do anything. Like how you're afraid of living a boring life," Cane elaborated, judgment heavy in their voice. "Going to work every day, coming home to just sit around and do nothing—"

"I don't do nothing," Etta pushed back.

Cane ignored her and continued, their voice growing more exaggerated. "Going to The Attic is not living. Sam's right. It's the recipe for mundanity. Spending your days staring at words and books is how people go crazy. I mean, just look at Dorian." Etta went to correct them but couldn't break through the rant. "Life on the road, now that's living! It's adventure. It's excitement!

"Nothing is tying us down. We can do whatever we want, whenever we want! And we can do this for as long as we want!"

"That doesn't sound sustainable," Etta remarked. "What about food and money?"

"Forget work! We can find odd jobs, enough to buy food and supplies and whatever else we could possibly need. And think about it—like really think about it—we don't need much."

Etta thought it over and grew silent. Part of it did sound appealing. She wouldn't have to sit in front of a computer every day. She wouldn't have to worry about her sunless bedroom in her apartment. She could step outside into one marvelous landscape after another, whenever she wanted. And it appeared to be the foolproof preventative measure to dodge reclusivity. It was an admittedly attractive idea. "Yeah, I guess."

The air was thick but still, looming overhead. Etta felt exposed. Bunching the sheets up around her neck, her thoughts sped through her mind, loud and boisterous, bright and flashy. The racing spread to her fingertips, compelling them to squirm and twitch. It traveled up her spine, tensing up her shoulders, and then down through her lower half. Straightening and stretching her legs, Etta desperately hoped for relief from the overwhelming feeling of bone on bone. Etta took a deep breath, followed by another and then another and another.

"Can't settle?" Cane's voice broke through the quiet. The anxious storm in Etta's mind momentarily parted, revealing the clear, grateful sky. They acknowledged her unease. Now they'd be able to correct it together.

"Same," Cane continued. "I'm just too excited for tomorrow and the coming days. There's so much we can do!"

Etta fought her rising disappointment. But it was going to be fine. She was also excited for tomorrow and whatever else the trip would bring. And they'd have to go home eventually. They still had jobs and responsibilities to get back to. But this was fine while Cane finished grieving. At least for now. Besides, Etta was the one to suggest getting away from Northampton. So she answered honestly, "Me either."

Cane rolled in to face Etta, their glee palpable through the night. "Should we crack open *Vox Libri*? We always sleep better after reading a passage."

Before Etta could object, Cane sat up and turned on the overhead light. They crawled to the front of the minivan and grabbed *Vox Libri* off the passenger seat. Etta sat straight, holding the blankets tightly against her body. A delirious smile stretched across Cane's face as they flipped through the pages and began to read.

As soon as Cane closed the book, it became bright outside. As if the night was quickly fast-forwarded. Curious as to what they would find, Etta crawled to the car door and slid it open. There lay a walkway leading up to a colorful Queen Anne home with a beautiful wrap-around porch and a turret to make Rapunzel jealous. Excited to explore, they scrambled out of the car and up to the door, knocking twice before stepping inside.

Etta pushed the door open and walked into the foyer. She instantly fell and landed limp and lifeless on the floor. Trying not to panic, she took a deep breath. This was what *Vox Libri* did. None of it was real. This was all in her head. Etta just needed to strap in and go along for the ride.

At least she could still move her eyes. They rolled in their sockets searching for Cane who was nowhere to be found. Etta noticed the unpainted walls adorned with portrait frames holding no pictures, and the ornately carved but unfinished furniture. But while everything was finely detailed, it was all made from the same cheap, flimsy wood, reminiscent of a dollhouse her grandmother bought her as a kid.

As Etta grew more still, cautiously ready to experience whatever *Vox Libri* had to show, she heard a deafening, metallic click as the house shook. The back wall slowly opened up like a giant door, its hinges squealing. Outside, Etta saw a giant torso. As fear overtook the false calm, sinking deeper into her motionless body, the torso lowered. Etta watched anxiously. A shoulder and then a neck, a chin, a cheek, and then an eye. Cane's eye. By the look of it, Cane was smiling— happy to be giant and happy to find Etta. Cane stood up and backed away slightly before their giant hand reached into the house, scooping up Etta by the waist.

As Etta's body hung limp in this new position, she caught sight of her arms and legs. Her skin was sallow like a pale, blond wood. The same wood that made up all the furniture and walls. The hair hanging in front of her eyes was too glossy, almost like plastic. But Etta was most petrified by the notches and screws at the crook of her joints. Every wrist, ankle, knee, elbow, and knuckle was fastened to her arms and legs by a tiny ball and screws. Cane held Etta up to their tremendous face and smiled. They flipped Etta over in their hand. Etta heard a cranking sound and then just as quickly as she lost her mobility, she was able to move again.

Cane set Etta back down into the house. Her mechanical hands flew to her face before frantically inspecting her body. Every joint was the same and her movement jerkily reflected as such. Reaching behind her, she felt a giant metal key attached to the center of her back. Etta desperately looked up to Cane who was still smiling back.

"Let's play!" Cane exclaimed before eagerly moving furniture pieces around.

Etta calmed down. She felt safe, even loved, as Cane gently held her in their hands. Cane moved her around the house, taking Etta from room to room, make-believing a busy day of chores. They giggled together as Cane put on a different voice, playing out an improvised script for her.

Soon enough, Etta felt herself winding down. Her joints were becoming more and more difficult to move. They were growing stiffer by the second. But Etta told herself not to worry. Deep down, she knew Cane would wind her back up.

She looked up at Cane whose smile was steadily shrinking. Cane lay Etta down on the floor and sat back staring. They looked bored. Etta tried forcing a smile, but she could no longer move. She fruitlessly tried calling out for Cane. Playtime didn't have to be over. They could wind Etta up and get back to it. Cane could give her life again. Etta waited for Cane to make a move, but as more time passed, they looked more detached.

Cane's head snapped toward a sound Etta couldn't hear. They stood up. Excitement flooded through Etta. This was it. Cane would pick her up, crank her key, and everything would be fun again. They walked out of Etta's periphery. She waited. *Patience*, Etta reminded herself. Hold tightly. Another moment or two. Keep calm. Cane wouldn't leave her like this. Stay brave. This would all end soon.

CHAPTER 18

———

"You're in San Francisco?" Sam yelled over the phone causing the unease to bubble in Etta's stomach. The roommates hadn't spoken in over ten days, not since their uncomfortable encounter before Etta left for The Attic.

"Technically," she began, her voice dragging more than usual, "I'm leaving San Francisco."

Sam's laugh resonated through the phone, loudly enough for Cane to overhear. Etta looked over, watching the amusement spread across Cane's face as they drove. She knew Cane took joy from the chaos and impulsivity of their trip, which she felt initially. However, the thrill was starting to lose its buzz. And she was officially drained.

"To be honest, I figured the two of you just U-Hauled or something and were too distracted living your bliss to call or text. But good for you. This is so out of your comfort zone! You needed some spice in your life!" Sam's encouragement pierced through her ears and echoed off the inside of her hollow body. Etta excused the feeling as sleep deprivation. She and Cane had read *Vox Libri* every night since Zion, and it was starting to take a toll on her. But without it, they both had trouble getting to sleep. "What'd you see so far?"

"We're currently on our way to..." Etta looked toward Cane for confirmation, "Muir Woods. We're gonna look at some giant redwoods."

"That's awesome! You're so lucky Valeska let the two of you take all this time off from work. I'm very jealous," Sam rambled. Etta didn't have it in her to tell him she failed to call in to work; that she and Cane essentially ran away and ignored every text or call. She desperately tried not to think about it. Because if she thought about it, her anxiety would rev up. And when her anxiety spurred, she became too distracted to appreciate everything around her. Instead, she let out a soft mm-hmm and let Sam continue.

Cane pulled past the ranger hut and found a parking spot. Looking over at Etta, they whispered something about running to the bathroom and filling up their water bottles. Etta gave a thumbs up and watched Cane climb out of the car.

"Any idea when you'll be back?" Sam asked. Etta didn't know how to answer the question. She and Cane never talked about how long they would be away. Nor did Cane give any indication of when. Etta originally figured they'd be away for a long weekend at most; that they'd stay pretty local until Cane was finished grieving over their high school friend. Etta was on board with that plan. But this was going on far longer than she'd expected. And their time away from home, and especially work, was already pushing it.

"Not really," she admitted. "But probably not for too much longer."

"You know what? I'm proud of you. A little spontaneity never hurt anybody. And we both know you needed it."

Etta quietly mm-hmmed Sam again as Cane climbed into the back of the van. "Hey, Sam? I gotta go. We just pulled into the park."

"Of course! Of course! Go have fun. Riley and I love and miss you—so does Cleese—but we'll see you soon!"

"Love you too," she replied, hanging up. Cane handed her a water bottle over their shoulder before tossing a few granola bars and other snacks into their backpacks. Etta laid it in her lap and looked at the dense woods ahead of them. From the base of the trunks to the tops she couldn't see, Etta beheld the unnaturally natural wonder of it all. Everything out west, it seemed, was taller, wider, overwhelmingly larger. She rested her head against the seat and closed her eyes.

"So we have a few different trail options," Cane blurted, startling Etta, "all of which seem pretty easy and not super long. But most are connected to each other, so we can be out for a while." Cane whipped out their map, leaned between the driver and passenger seats, and drew a route with their fingertips. "If we start with the main trail, it eventually comes to a bridge, which we can bypass, continue on the Bootjack Trail in the neighboring state park, and go down the TCC Trail, which will lead us to the Ben Johnson that brings us back to the same bridge. Sound good?"

"And long."

"Great!" Cane exclaimed, folding up the map and putting it back in their bag. "Let's get going!"

Lifting her head off the seat, Etta picked up her water bottle and lazily unscrewed the top. She held Cane's gaze as she leisurely sipped. Cane held their bag in front of them, their eyes widening with impatience. Etta's gritted restraint wore thin. She was exhausted.

"Before we go, I want to check the rest of my messages," Etta stated.

"Sure, go ahead, I guess," Cane responded, their voice saturated with irritation as they climbed back out of the van. Etta shut her eyes and ignored it, listening for the door to roll shut. Phone in hand, Etta feigned scrolling. She just needed another minute to rest, but with Cane standing outside her door, Etta assumed they were watching.

Opening up her texts, Etta noticed she had service and had multiple unread messages. Some from Sam, a few from her mother and sister, and many from Valeska. Guilt struck hard like a pickaxe hitting an oil pipe, allowing the inner muck to spill out. Etta closed her texts and opened her email instead. She still wasn't ready to leave the car. Her inbox was full of emails from Valeska. Many subject headers contained question marks or phrases mentioning vacation and sick leave. The top read *Termination: Effective Immediately.*

The sludge in her stomach hardened, forming a solid mass. It pushed against the rest of her organs and made it difficult to breathe. Terminated? As in fired? As in she was no longer employed by Brain Train?

Etta jumped out of the car and held her phone up to Cane's face.

"I'm fired!" she shrieked, scrunching her face to avoid crying. Cane stood unconcerned and unmoved, their face stone. "I'm fired. I... ruined it. I lost. I lost time. I spent months working toward something different. Anything. Anywhere. It didn't matter where.

"And I made headway. I made progress," Etta continued. "I was working hard, and I moved forward. And now that time is lost and was for nothing. Now I'll have to start over again."

Etta threw herself into Cane's arms and buried her head in the crook of their neck. She could feel her tears dripping off her cheek and onto Cane's shoulder, and she felt embarrassed. She was getting Cane's shoulder wet, and that must have been uncomfortable—all because Etta worked hard. Then threw it away. Almost intentionally. At first, it didn't even cross her mind. Cane was in pain and needed to get away, and where Cane was, so was *Vox Libri*. So it was a nonissue to get away. But then the trip stretched out longer than expected, and even though Etta did notice the unease brewing beneath the surface, it was easy to ignore after cracking open *Vox Libri*.

Her phone would ring and vibrate, but shame pushed through her nerves. And more days would flip by like a page on a Rolodex calendar, and the embarrassment made it harder for Etta to move her arms. To get her brain to send the signal through her nervous system to her hands and fingers to answer the phone.

Etta's cheek was damp. Her tears had officially soaked through Cane's shirt enough to wet her cheek. Etta sniffed, stood straighter, and then let out a snort as she wiped down Cane's shoulder.

"I'm so sorry," Etta sorrowfully laughed holding the bridge of her nose. "It's just... I worked so hard to be sent back to the beginning."

She looked up at Cane, still vacant and wooden, and Etta grew confused. "Wh—Why don't you seem surprised? Or rattled?"

"Well," they muttered, taking a step back but still keeping their hands on Etta's shoulders, "I figured as much."

"You figured as much? What does that mean?"

Cane stepped back, pulling their own phone out of their back pocket. They scrolled for a moment before showing it to Etta. "I got the same email two days ago. I just assumed if I got it, you got one too."

As if a switch flipped, Etta's posture grew taller. A chilling resolve crystallized itself in her chest, flash-freezing everything from her body to her mind with a frigid clarity, an icy cognizance. "You've been sitting on this for two days, and you didn't bother to say anything?"

"Not for nothing," Cane began, "but what did you expect?"

Etta bore her eyes into Cane whose face melted into a patronizing faux sympathy. They came closer and wrapped Etta up in a tight hug. "Oh, sweetie, I didn't realize you'd be this upset!" Cane fussed, rubbing her back. "I didn't realize you cared about the job this much."

"I liked it enough to care whether I got fired," Etta replied, her voice softening. "And I liked Valeska enough to care about what she thought of me."

Cane loosened their grip around Etta and snickered. "Well, ya don't gotta worry about that last bit anymore. Besides, now we can keep adventuring! We've got nothing tying us down!"

Etta felt frozen in place as her surroundings faded. The vibrant greens of the trees were desaturated and the sun above dulled. The static resonating in her head drowned out the rustle of the wind and chatter of the hikers. She was barely aware of Cane cupping her cheeks and laying a kiss on her forehead. And Etta only vaguely noticed as Cane grabbed her hand and began leading her toward the trailhead.

Overhead hung a wooden sign held up by large logs and two rusty chains. Leafy trees lined the trail, one right after the other, revealing nothing but more green beyond the row. Each step echoed off the boardwalk beneath them, reverberating off the empty walls of Etta's mind. As they moved farther down the path, the trees grew larger. The trunks were wider, and it was becoming even more impossible to see the tops of the trees. Cane remarked how they felt like they ate a cake from Wonderland and then pulled Etta over to one of the more colossal, hollowed-out trees. They forced Etta into the opening, stepped back, and snapped a picture. Etta wasn't even sure she smiled.

Cane giggled to themself, gesturing for Etta to join them, but she was still unable to move. At every shift or turn, she was met with an invisible resistance like swimming through an ocean with a heavy current. Cane jogged over and took her hand before continuing to guide her along. A child holding a banana slug bound in front of them, eager to show her sister, and stopped them in their tracks. Cane's chuckle brought some sensory awareness back to Etta.

Fired. She had no job. How would she be able to pay rent? How would she be able to feed herself? What did she have to come home to now? Nothing, really. To Cane's point, nothing was stopping her from staying in Muir Woods forever.

Etta looked overhead and fully saw the enormity of the forest. She felt small. Too small. She felt unreal. The last time she'd felt this fake, she'd turned into a doll and was left stock-still on a dollhouse floor. Her muscles stiffened and frenzy rooted itself in her chest, creeping its way across her nerves. Etta pulled her hand from Cane's and inspected it. She wasn't made of wood, but the metamorphosis feeling was taking hold. Shaking her hands like they were wet, Etta tried to keep hold of any sensation, but she began feeling a thin string snaking around her ankles and up her legs. She could hear the chime of keys clanging together, the sound of a kite resisting the wind, the hiss of a snare drum, and the croon of a horn. The sky darkened and the brewing storm charged the air.

"I can't," Etta whispered to herself, bringing her hands up to her hair and compressing her temples with her wrists. Shrinking to the ground, Etta pulled her knees in tightly and closed the back of her throat to stop from screaming. Her body temperature rose as sweat clung to her shirt and back. A hand rested gently on her shoulder. Her eyes followed it up the arm to see Cane looking scared.

"I can't. I can't," Etta continued muttering, allowing gravity to win and lying on her side. Cane cradled her head, laying it in their lap. She could hear Cane's voice, but they were far away and underwater. Etta let out a whispered scream forceful enough to scratch her throat and then cried, "I'm just so tired."

CHAPTER 19

———

The bedroom was as dark as it always was in the daytime. The tree outside her window blocked the sun from breaking through. The blankets twisted around Etta's legs like a cocoon, but she was comfortable. And she was resting. And her brain was finally quiet.

Sam knocked on the door and then let himself in without waiting for an answer. He carried a sandwich on a paper plate, set it down on the nightstand, and then sat next to Etta on the bed. She looked up at him and smiled before sitting up.

"You didn't have to bring me food," Etta started, her voice hoarse.

Sam lay his hand on her leg, trying to smile through his furrowed brow. "It's been three days," he replied, "and all you've done since you got home was sleep."

Etta pulled her blanketed knees up to her chest and wrapped her arms around them. Her bedroom felt unreal. The apartment felt unreal. She'd spent weeks in both fantasy worlds and unbelievable landscapes, and now she was back in her bed. Jobless.

Her under-eyes felt puffy and raw, and her muscles were

stiff. She tried ignoring the dull headache from being horizontal for too long and pulled her hair out of its ponytail. Using her fingertips, she massaged her scalp to alleviate some of the pressure. "Dissociation is a hell of a drug."

Sam scooted himself closer and gave Etta a tight hug. "Did you and Cane fight? What happened?"

"Long story short, I'm not cut out for big adventure," Etta explained before telling Sam the ins and outs of her tumultuous trip. "And to make matters worse," she continued, laying her head on her knees, "I lost my job."

She expected herself to cry. Etta figured she would when she said it all out loud. In a matter of weeks, she managed to make a new friend, become romantically involved with them, hurt her relationship with another friend, become dependent on escapism for the sake of life experience, run away to live life on the road, and finally, get fired. But the fatigue was too great and Etta was too dehydrated to produce any more tears.

Etta expected Sam to begin comforting her and was surprised when he didn't. She pulled her head up from her knees and looked over at her roommate. Instead of looking concerned or sympathetic, he appeared guilty. His eyes were cast to the side, and his shoulders were in an almost cowering position.

"What?" Etta asked, her frustration building.

Sam kept his eyes down and dismissively flipped his hand. "No, nothing," he brushed off.

She sat up taller and crossed her legs. Sam's eyes, filled with sheepish shame and pity, met hers. Adamant to find out, Etta pushed further. "No, really. What's going on?"

"It's good news, actually," he said, his voice timid. "Riley asked me to move in with him."

If Etta sat any straighter, her back would have snapped in half. She liked Riley. She knew he made Sam happy. And she loved Sam, who deserved to be happy. But losing her home on top of the other accrued misfortunes wasn't on her Bad Luck Bingo card, yet here she was.

"I realize now's probably not the best time to tell you, but our lease is up in two months anyway. And sure, we're moving pretty fast, but it feels like the right time."

Her eyes began to well up with the tears she thought she no longer had. Of course, she was happy for them. But without Sam and now jobless, she wasn't sure how she'd be able to make the rent, which meant she would probably have to move elsewhere. And find a new job.

She thought she was settled. Etta thought she'd found a steady job and a secure place to live. And now, in less than a year, she'd mucked everything up. She was further behind than from where she started.

Wiping away a tear, Etta forced a smile. "I'm sorry," she stammered. "I'm happy for you two. I really am. This is all just a lot."

Sam leaned over to wrap his arm around her. Etta laid her head in the crook of his neck, letting out a few sobs, her tears soaking through his shirt. Sam rubbed her back and tried calming her down. His soft hums were broken by the intermittent shushing and the occasional, "It'll be okay."

"I know. I know," Etta continued, lifting her head off of Sam. "Everything's just moving so damn fast. I wish it could all slow down for a single minute so I can catch my breath."

"This isn't going to change anything between us. You know that. Right? We'll still be friends and you can come over or out with us whenever you'd like!"

"I know. I know."

"And besides," Sam continued, standing up from the bed, "you're not going to be alone. You've got Cane now."

The hollow throb pulsated in her empty stomach. Sam was right. It was going to be okay. Logic told her that. And he was right in saying Etta wouldn't be alone. She had Cane now. She felt the need to apologize to Cane. For what, she was unsure of. But Etta needed to make amends and make sure they were still okay. Everything would be okay. She was going to be okay. Things needed to be okay.

Etta looked up at Sam and forced another smile. She beckoned him to come back over to the bed and then threw her arms around his neck, clinging tightly. "I promise. I am so happy for you guys."

Sam shimmied his way out, smiled back at his roommate, and then pointed to the sandwich. "Please eat something."

Etta nodded as he backed out of her room and shut the door behind him. As she rubbed her eyes, her stomach rumbled, but she didn't have an appetite. However, grateful Sam put in the effort, she reached for the unsavory white bread and turkey sandwich, took a bite, and swallowed. Fighting back a grimace, she forced half of it down, leaving the rest on her bedside table before grabbing her phone.

Overwhelmed by the check-in message Cane sent after dropping her off at home—to which she didn't reply—Etta stared at the blinking cursor of the empty message box. She'd ignored everything and everyone once she got back. She didn't have the energy. And that was still true, but she needed to start collecting the leftover bits of her Northampton life. She knew that much.

Are you busy? Etta typed. *Ironically, I need a change of scenery.*

On the bus ride over to Cane's apartment, Etta mentally rehearsed what to say and how to say it while preparing responses to hypothetical questions: *I was tired. I was overwhelmed. But I was trying to be supportive through your grief.* Vox Libri *made me oversensitive in a strange place. It was a bad idea bringing it with us. But maybe we can read another passage now?*

The sun found a break through the overcast sky, warming the top of Etta's head as she walked through Cane's garden. Standing at the back door, she unbuttoned her jacket and loosened her colorful scarf. She took a deep breath and rang the rusty doorbell.

"It's unlocked!" Etta heard Cane call from deep within their apartment.

Opening the door, Etta walked into the kitchen. Unconstructed cardboard boxes lying on the table and open cabinet doors with empty shelves greeted her. She stepped carefully over containers filled with Cane's pots, pans, plates, bowls, and other kitchenware. Etta pushed into the living room, finding Cane sitting on the floor wrapping their bookshelf trinkets in newspaper. She paused in the doorway, her practiced explanation corroding into nothing more than a useless rock pile of thoughts.

"Are you purging or something?" Etta asked with a slight laugh, stepping deeper into the chaos.

Cane avoided meeting Etta's eyes, their grip tightening on a tiny model airplane. Reaching for another sheet of newspaper, they wrapped the plane and placed it in an open box next to them.

"I… I'm not cut out for…" Cane gazed at the boxes and then looked back at Etta. "The happiest I've ever been was when we were traveling—constantly moving and meeting new people and seeing new things. Grilling over a campfire, drinking coffee in random shops in random cities, pushing our sleeping bags together because it was cold. That's what I want to do."

Etta stood coolly. The barely addressed fatigue prevented her from reacting or feeling a reaction. She figured Cane was enjoying their time on the road more than she was, but she was distracted from how much more. "I mean, yeah. It was fun, but didn't you get tired? Didn't you miss your own bed?"

Laying their hands in their lap, Cane cast their gaze downward while Etta waited. And her impatience multiplied. Initially inconsequential and then more prominent the longer Cane took to reply.

"I can't stay in Northampton," they conceded. "Or Massachusetts, for that matter."

"Wait… What are you getting at?" Etta asked.

The room felt vacuum sealed without a single sound. The air felt thinner, becoming difficult to breathe. The boxes made sense. Cane was packing. Cane was leaving. Like everyone and everything else. The last bit of her new life's foundation was also crumbling away.

"So you're just going to pick up and go?" Etta pressed, her volume increasing. "What are you going to do for money and food? Where are you going to sleep?"

"I'll figure it out. It's not like I have a job lined up here anyway," Cane ribbed. "Besides, there are always odd jobs everywhere and hostels and a surprising number of people opening up their homes to strangers outside of the States. I'll be okay."

Staring at Cane, Etta felt far away from them. Every sentence added another ten feet until Etta was on one side of the tunnel and Cane on the other. Their hollow words echoed against the cavernous walls. Etta lost her balance and caught herself against the doorframe. From her periphery, Cane quietly watched.

"But what am I going to do?" Etta muttered, still too dehydrated to produce any tears. "You're just going to leave me here alone?"

Cane didn't move. Etta glared, waiting for them to speak. Waiting for them to stand. Waiting for them to move in the slightest. Impatiently, she continued. "Sam is moving out with Riley. You know I don't have a job either. And I suspect Dorian's mad at me."

Cane sat a moment longer before excitedly shooting up. They rushed over to Etta, wrapping their arms around her shoulders. "Then come with me! Pack up your shit. We'll throw it in the back of my car and we'll travel together. We did it before. We can totally do it again!"

Etta glared at the inconsiderate suggestion. "Were we on the same trip? Were you not standing next to me at Muir Woods? What makes you think I'm not just ready, but willing to do that again?"

"Because it's absolutely doable!" Cane exclaimed, springing back toward the boxes and stack of newspaper. "It can be you and me against the world. All of that cliché crap we read about all the time. If anybody can do it, we can. Etta, we can be happy together on the road."

Etta stepped back in disbelief. "I'm sorry, but what? What the fuck are you actually talking about?"

"Us. Traveling together. Being together. We can do it and we can be happy instead of being stuck in this boring place."

"Cane," Etta started, trying to reason with them. "No. That's not a thing. And when has there ever been an 'us'? When did we ever establish an 'us'? It's always been that 'who knows what the future holds' bullshit."

Cane looked confused. "What do you mean? It's always been 'us.' It's you and me. You and me and coffee and *Vox Libri* and the minivan and words. It's us. It's our path."

"What path?" Etta yelled pushing herself off the wall and closer to the couch. "Do you mean your ridiculous notions of pretending to be a modern-day beatnik? Because that's not a thing. It's all well and good to travel and see things and be adventurous, but what about the comfort of routine?"

"I thought this was something we both wanted..."

"When have I ever expressed that?"

"We talk about it all the time!"

"No," Etta continued, putting her hand on Cane's chest to keep them at a distance as they neared. "You talk about it all the time. And I always say the same thing—that it's a nice idea, but it's nothing more than a story. It's not real. It's a distraction."

Holding Etta's eye contact, Cane stood taller and raised their head. "*Vox Libri*'s a distraction. You don't seem to have a lot to say about that."

An invisible vortex spontaneously absorbed the imagined tunnel filling the room and the distance Etta felt disappeared with it. Short and shallow breaths kept her standing, but she knew she was moments away from collapsing.

"Am I a distraction too?" Cane continued unblinking.

Gritting her teeth, Etta forced the only response manageable. "That's not fair."

Standing silently in the living room, Etta's thoughts reeled with the realization they'd been living two different narratives for longer than either realized. It was just that; talk. But apparently, she was wrong. They were serious about it all. And what was worse, Etta thought Cane was right. All of it was a distraction. A diversion from mundanity. Nothing more than a magic trick.

Etta wiped a frustrated tear off of her cheek and sniffed. "So you're leaving?"

Standing in front of her, Cane cast their eyes to the side. "And you're staying."

Etta nodded. "Do you know when or if you'll be back?"

Cane shook their head then looked back at Etta.

"I'm going to miss you," Etta whispered walking closer and pulling Cane into a tight hug.

Cane hugged her back tightly, kissing her hair before laying their head on hers. She could hear their voice cracking. "I can't believe you're not coming with me."

Etta held back the few angry words remaining but thought against it. "Promise you won't disappear entirely?"

CHAPTER 20

———

Etta walked hard to The Attic, grinding resentment into the pavement. She couldn't offer Cane a hand with packing. She couldn't stomach it. So she went home to a note from Sam explaining he and Cleese were sleeping over Riley's. As Etta plopped on the couch, relief and stillness surprised her. For the first time in a long time, she couldn't hear the static or the storm or the clanging or the guttural screaming. And it was soothing.

Nearing The Attic door, Etta tightened her grip around the strap of her backpack, prepping herself for the reintroduction. This was the longest she'd gone without visiting the shop. Which, when she reflected, was only a few weeks, but recently, each exit outdid itself in unfavorability.

The door squawked as she pushed it open. Etta wasn't positive, but it felt lighter. Maybe that was in her head, though. She spotted Dorian flipping through an old book, gingerly holding each page between his fingertips. Etta approached the counter, waiting for him to look up.

"If you're going to browse, be very careful with the books. Some of them are centuries old and worth more than your entire lifetime." His voice was stern. Setting her backpack on the floor, Etta smirked. She could always count on Dorian to stay surly. Cautiously leaning on the counter, she strained to get a better look at his book.

"I was actually hoping to catch up," she replied.

Dorian sat back on his stool, looking up from the book and directly at Etta, smiling slightly. "It's been a while," he stated, crossing his arms without appearing pressed or bitter or offended. "Where've you been?"

Relaying the condensed version of the tale, Etta watched Dorian's subtle reactions. At the mention of *Vox Libri*, his eyes perked up, so she continued telling him everything she saw. "They were beyond sensational—enchanting and magical, freeing but also terrifying. But the exhaustion that followed was so draining. I'm sure that's what put me over the edge."

"Many enchanted books are out there," Dorian stated, pushing his glasses up to the top of his head. "And they can really mess you up if you're not careful."

"So why didn't you warn me about it?" Etta asked.

Dorian shrugged. "You asked me about a book. I found the book. I showed you the book. I tried preventing you from taking the book home, but your paramour made it seem like the two of you knew what you were getting yourselves into. Speaking of, where are they?"

"Moving." Etta expected a pang or a stabbing sensation, but she felt nothing other than the same stillness from the night before. "Wanderlust was too alluring."

"How're they going to pull that off? What about work?"

Etta spoke cautiously and slowly, hesitant for Dorian's judgment. "Because we were away for so long, we lost our jobs. Both of us. They're going to find 'odd jobs' on the road, and I'm now unemployed and alone because my roommate is moving out, so I soon won't be able to afford my rent."

Etta felt embarrassment trying to swarm her, but acceptance proved itself a reliable deterrent. She shrugged and continued. "But enough about me. I came here to disengage from the outside. What about you? What are you up to?" Etta asked, walking around the counter to get another better look at Dorian's book.

Dorian pulled open the drawer underneath the register and handed her a pair of gloves. The book looked like a sacred, religious text—grand, ornamented with golden inlay and gilded edges swept open. Motioning for Etta to come closer, Dorian pointed to a word in the middle of the page.

"You're probably out of practice," he joked. Etta scoffed and rolled her eyes. "But this should be an easy one."

Leaning over, Etta followed Dorian's finger. "Really? *Resiliēns?*"

Dorian chuckled, warming Etta's insides. She was grateful for the normalcy and Dorian's willingness to encourage, comfort, and distract her.

"Okay, fine," he continued. Dorian delicately picked up a section of pages and gently turned them. She watched as he skimmed the text, using his finger as a guide before landing on a new one. "What about this one?"

"*Opportūnitās?* As in 'opportunity'?"

The door opened, distracting the pair and breaking their concentration. A young person with short hair and glasses walked in without stepping too far into the store. Etta and Dorian watched the amazement settle on the new face as they beheld the store. The young patron timidly walked to the counter.

"Excuse me?" they gently interrupted. "I'm trying to start collecting books. Can I ask a few questions?"

Etta looked over at Dorian, turning away from the customer. He gestured toward Etta. "She can help you."

Expectantly looking at Etta, their eagerness grew. Side-eyeing Dorian, Etta stepped from behind the counter to help the new client. They rambled on about an ornate hardcover series of classic fiction they remembered from their grandfather's library. They described the covers in great detail and mentioned ogling them whenever they visited The Attic.

Etta guided them through the store, directing them to a shelf stacked with books of a similar description before making her way back. Still standing behind the counter, Dorian shut the book and smugly removed his glasses.

"I know you hate people," Etta began, "but as you've pointed out before, I don't work here."

"Do you want to?" Dorian asked.

"What? Why?"

"You're better with the clientele—far better than I could ever be. Or really, ever want to be." He smiled. "Besides, I want to focus on estate sales and my restoration projects. If you manned the store, I could do that."

Etta stood stunned. Accepting Dorian's offer felt like accepting the life Cane and Sam feared. But curiosity stirred throughout her body. Different thoughts and feelings sped through her mind like horses at the Kentucky Derby. A shotgun blast and off they went. Hesitation was off the pace and Endearment eased. Caution spit the bit, falling behind Relief. But Objection and Surrender held on for the ultimate photo finish.

The young customer walked up to the counter with six large, gilded books in hand. They lay the books down on the counter and let out a huge breath like someone who'd just run a marathon. Dorian stood up from his stool, cradling his book under his arm. Looking at Etta, he smiled again and then headed toward the office stairs.

Etta stepped back behind the counter, pulling the books closer to the register.

"I can ring you up."

ACKNOWLEDGMENTS

Over the years it took to get here, *Vox Libri* has collected a menagerie of wonderfully unique friends, mentors, supporters, and cheerleaders. I still can't comprehend the level of love and encouragement you've all shown me, especially when I couldn't believe I deserved it.

First and foremost, thank you to my family for being storytellers themselves—whether or not they recognize it. Your love of sharing jokes, anecdotes, and other one-offs is how I fell in love with the art of storytelling to begin with. Thank you for never trying to scare me away from the field of literature and for allowing me the time and space to finally finish this project.

A big thank you to my Bitchachas for both just being there and taking me on the best adventures ever. The warmest gratitude to my partner for being my calm throughout the storm. As well as a big shout out to Beer Club and my Bingo group for keeping me sane and grounded while we were stuck in our homes.

To my Beta Readers—Amelia, Grace, Christina, and Ali—whether you've been with Etta from the start or only just met her, you helped guide her out of the attic and bring her story to life for which I will be eternally grateful!

A special acknowledgment goes to the FDU Creative Writing Department—specifically David Grand—for forcing me to take my abstract idea and give it a proper structure with characters, plot, and setting. And an even greater acknowledgment to the Book Creators and New Degree Press teams —Eric Koester, Brian Bies, ChandaElaine Spurlock, Ilia Epifanov, and Mozelle Jordan—for teaching me how to properly apply my book writing skills.

I must also thank the most magical Bibliophiles an author can ask for. Your generosity made *Vox Libri* real. Your patience allowed me the time I needed to officially finish this manuscript. And your endless support got me through to the end. Thank you to the following: Shana Abraham, Joanne Accardi-Goldberger, Maggie Alfaro, Deanna Amodeo, Tina Armenti, Rhiannon Auriemma, Amanda Bashford, Devina Bhalla, Melanie Boyne, Melanie Bussiere, Franchesca Chabla, Anwesha Chadhuri, Dan Clavijo, Phyllis Collyer, Kevin Cosenza, Anthony Costa, Eric & Michelle Couper, Maria Cunha, Jessica Dahmer, Dawn Dahmer, Margaret Danko, Saransh Desai-Chowdhry, Maureen Devine-Ahl, Ilia Epifanov, Amelia Fisher, Angelly Fitzpatrick, Michael Fountain, Venice Franco, Jill Fredenburg, Joy Frisoli, Lauren Frisoli, Joanne Genzanto, Stephanie Gillespie, Luz Gillette, Patricia Giramma, Mirna Giron, Mary Lou Gugger, Kelly Gugger, Debarun Gupta, Ian Hassan, Marie Elena Hasson, Grace Hasson, Andrea Hayes, Dawn Hedgecock, Rita Howley, Fidel

Kargbo, Rose Kargbo, Gabriella Kenny, Erica Kidder, Donte Kirby, Gloria Kitchens, Anthony Klick, Eric Koester, Sue Kollias, Frank Krov, Lisette LaForge, Angellica Lardieri, Heidi Lauer, Christine Lauer, Jennifer Lauer, Lillian Li, Matt Lonergan, Christine Lopez, Gianmarco Masoni, Donna Masucci, Christina Masucci, Darby McCarthy, Alejandra McNeil, AJ Mokes, Kathy Mooney, Jessica Nikithser, Cady North, Lynn Olson, Kristen Olson, Kris Orsini, Sharon Podobnik Peterson, Andrea Powell, Justin Rizzi, Kit Rubino, Meaghan Rush, Doris Sew Hoy, Ahmed Siddiqui, Alexa C Smith, ChandaElaine Spurlock, Cassandra Stirling, Chrissa Stulpin, Katarvia Taylor, Catherine Trapani, Maggie Trapani, Sharon Uyar, Marcella Vineis, Keri Vornadore, Jordan Waterwash, Bernadette Watson, Elaine Weaver, Kayla Weinerman, Lisa Wellet, Mark Wellet, Sandra Wellet, Stephanie Wellet, Julie Willis, Rose Marie Zarillo, Susanne N Zebro, Sarah Zebro, and Mark Zebro, Jr—I adore you all.

And finally, thank you to John Koenig and *The Dictionary of Obscure Sorrows*. Discovering your blog in 2013 was my *keyframe*. You made me feel heard when I, *hem-jawed*, couldn't find the words. Without your hard work, creativity, and passion for language, *Vox Libri* wouldn't exist. May our collective *mahpiohanzia* one day be satiated.

APPENDIX

Epigraph

Koenig, John. *The Dictionary of Obscure Sorrows*. New York: Simon & Schuster, 2021.

Author's Note

Anonymous. *Beowulf*, lines 1-3 + 11. Poetry Foundation, 2022. https://www.poetryfoundation.org/poems/43521/beowulf-old-english-version.

Koenig, John. *The Dictionary of Obscure Sorrows (blog)*, 2009-2022. https://www.dictionaryofobscuresorrows.com/.

Schweizer, S., R. A Kievit, T. Emery, Cam-CAN, and R. N. Henson. "Symptoms of Depression in a Large Healthy Population Cohort Are Related to Subjective Memory Complaints and Memory Performance in Negative Contexts." *Psychological Medicine*, Cambridge University Press, Jan. 2018. https://www.ncbi.nlm.nih.gov/pmc/articles/PMC5729845/.